'*Autobiographical Memory and the Self* is that rare work in psychology that provides a synthesis across subfields that is both theoretically original and of immediate practical value to the clinician. By demonstrating the powerful role of memory in ongoing thought, emotion, and motivation, the authors illustrate the centrality of remembered experience in goal definition and goal pursuit. Taking this a step further, they provide research on the linkage of autobiographical memory recall to both well-being and psychological disorder. Finally, they provide concrete evidence for how attention to memory processes can be a critical factor in the healing work of practitioners. This book is essential reading for both researchers and therapists.'

Jefferson A. Singer, Ph.D., Dean of the College, Faulk Foundation Professor of Psychology, Connecticut College, USA

Autobiographical Memory and the Self

Autobiographical memory shapes our understanding of ourselves, guides our behaviour, and helps us to develop and maintain relationships with others. The ways in which we interpret and narrate our memories have important implications for our psychological well-being, and can sometimes contribute to the onset and maintenance of a variety of psychological disorders.

Autobiographical Memory and the Self: Relationship and Implications for Cognitive-Behavioural Therapy synthesises the growing cognitive, social, personality, and clinical psychological literature on the memory-self relationship. It creates an interdisciplinary dialogue which explores autobiographical memory and its relevance for clinical practice, especially cognitive-behavioural therapy (CBT).

The authors propose a model for understanding the mechanisms of change involved in therapeutic interventions targeting negative or traumatic memories whilst providing insights into recent debates and avenues for future research. *Autobiographical Memory and the Self* will be useful to clinicians and clinical trainees, researchers, and psychology postgraduate students.

Soljana Çili is Lecturer in Psychology at the University of the Arts London and a visiting academic at the University of Southampton, UK. Her research focuses on the memory-imagery-self relationship.

Lusia Stopa is Professor of Clinical Psychology at the University of Southampton, UK. Her research examines how imagery represents the self and how imagery interventions can change negative self-views.

Autobiographical Memory and the Self

Relationship and Implications for Cognitive-Behavioural Therapy

Soljana Çili and Lusia Stopa

 Routledge
Taylor & Francis Group

LONDON AND NEW YORK

First published 2019
by Routledge
4 Park Square, Milton Park, Abingdon, Oxon OX14 4RN

and by Routledge
605 Third Avenue, New York, NY 10017

First issued in paperback 2022

Routledge is an imprint of the Taylor & Francis Group, an informa business

© 2019 Soljana Çili and Lusia Stopa

Publisher's Note
The publisher has gone to great lengths to ensure the quality of this reprint but points out that some imperfections in the original copies may be apparent.

British Library Cataloguing-in-Publication Data
A catalogue record for this book is available from the British Library

Library of Congress Cataloging-in-Publication Data
Names: Çili, Soljana, author. | Stopa, Lusia Aldona, 1954– author.
Title: Autobiographical memory and the self : relationship and implications for cognitive-behavioural therapy / Soljana Çili and Lusia Stopa.
Description: Abingdon, Oxon ; New York, NY : Routledge, 2019. | Includes index.
Identifiers: LCCN 2018018233 (print) | LCCN 2018021094 (ebook) | ISBN 9781351606103 (Adobe) | ISBN 9781351606080 (Mobipocket) | ISBN 9781351606097 (ePub) | ISBN 9781138093010 (hardback) | ISBN 9781315107103 (ebook)
Subjects: LCSH: Autobiographical memory. | Self. | Cognitive therapy. Classification: LCC BF378.A87 (ebook) | LCC BF378.A87 C495 2019 (print) | DDC 153.1/3–dc23
LC record available at https://lccn.loc.gov/2018018233

ISBN 13: 978-1-03-247611-7 (pbk)
ISBN 13: 978-1-138-09301-0 (hbk)
ISBN 13: 978-1-315-10710-3 (ebk)

DOI: 10.4324/9781315107103

Typeset in Times New Roman
by Out of House Publishing

To my parents, Suzana and Ferdinant Çili, and my sisters, Egla and Nikolina

SÇ

To my husband, Bruce Hunt and my children Chloe and James Stopa-Hunt for all their support

LS

Contents

Acknowledgements   x

Introduction   xi

1 Introduction to autobiographical memory
   and its functions   1

2 The journey from concrete experience to abstract
   self-knowledge: How autobiographical memory
   contributes to the development of the self   16

3 Not just a long-term affair: How autobiographical
   memory retrieval exerts an immediate influence
   on the self   38

4 Implications of the memory-self relationship for
   psychological well-being   55

5 Implications of the memory-self relationship and
   narrative identity literature for cognitive-behavioural
   therapy   93

6 What next? Reflections and directions for future
   research on the memory-self relationship   116

Index   126

Acknowledgements

We would like to thank the staff at Routledge, especially Ceri McLardy (our Editor) and Sophie Crowe (Editorial Assistant), for their support. I, Soljana, am grateful to Professors Dan P. McAdams and Jonathan M. Adler for answering my questions at various stages of the writing and to Professor Jefferson A. Singer for providing valuable suggestions for Chapter 4.

Introduction

In April 2016, media outlets such as *The Independent* and *Vanity Fair* reported a statement made days earlier by Sir Ian McKellen at the Oxford Literary Festival, United Kingdom. Talking about the memoirs he had initially agreed to write for a British publishing house, he reportedly stated:

> I put nine months aside to do it, and I got a very handsome advance. Then I sent the money back... It was a bit painful. I didn't want to go back into my life and imagine things that I hadn't understood so far.
>
> (Oppenheim, 2016)

While for some people this may have been simply a curious piece of news (the advance Sir Ian had returned was, after all, rumoured to be around £1 million), for anyone who has a painful past or just happens to be a memory researcher, Sir Ian's decision made sense. Fortunately or unfortunately, the past does not stay in the past. It shapes our personality, colours our views of ourselves and the world around us, and affects our emotions and how we behave or interact with our environment. As such, our past accompanies us in the present and shapes our future for better or worse. When it involves negative experiences, thinking about it can be painful and may be best avoided – even when you are offered £1 million to do it!

Memory has attracted scholars' attention for centuries. In fact, some modern conceptualisations of memory have much in common with arguments made by Socrates and Aristotle (see Bloch, 2007; Ricoeur, 2004). The interest in memory – especially autobiographical memory (AM) – grew significantly in 17th-century Europe, where social and economic changes led to a weakening of the extended family structure and to the rise of an individualistic culture that viewed individuals as autonomous and distinct from their social context (see Nelson, 2003). This was reflected at the time in the growing interest in individuals' unique life stories, for example those presented in novels and biographies. It continued to develop further into the 19th century, when there was an increased sense of conflict between the individual and society that resulted from social, economic, and political unrest and that led to a growing focus on the need for individuals to define their own selves and purposes in life (see Baumeister, 1987). Further social transformations occurring in the 20th and 21st centuries intensified the interest in memory. The last decades, in particular, have witnessed a worldwide rise in individualism, potentially as a result of factors (e.g., socioeconomic development and reduced infectious disease prevalence) that have contributed to a reduction in individuals' need to rely on their social groups (see Santos, Varnum, & Grossmann, 2017). In some countries this has been accompanied by a shift towards *personalism*, a culture in which one's needs and values are seen as independent of the social context and in which everyone "must have a personal story to tell... and everyone's story must emphasise his or her unique individuality" (Nelson, 2003, p. 133).

This growing interest in memory, accompanied by technological advances and enhanced research methods, has contributed to the growth of memory research in the last decades. Among the disciplines that have investigated memory are cognitive, social, personality, and clinical psychology. While some cognitive psychologists have focused on memory processes and structure (e.g., encoding, storage, retrieval), others (together with social and personality psychologists) have investigated memory functions. Social and personality psychologists have also focused on how AM influences the self and personality development, emotions, cognitions, and behaviours. Clinical psychologists, on the other hand, have mostly investigated how adverse memories and associated mental images contribute to the development and maintenance of psychological disorders and how they can be addressed in therapy, especially in cognitive-behavioural therapy (CBT). All this work has led to a proliferation of research articles, journal special issues, and books on AM. Although researchers and practitioners are drawing from each other's work to a certain extent, we believe that greater communication between disciplines is needed. In particular, we think that cognitive, social, and personality psychologists may benefit from a better understanding of the role of AM in psychopathology. Among other things, this can help them understand better the implications of their work. Meanwhile, clinical psychologists may benefit from the research on AM functions and on the memory-self relationship. This could improve their understanding of the experiences of patients who have gone through traumatic events and help them refine the therapeutic interventions they use with such patients. *This* is where our book comes in.

The aim of this book is to facilitate the dialogue between the different disciplines by synthesising the growing cognitive, social, personality, and clinical psychological literature on the memory-self relationship and its relevance for clinical practice. The idea is to put together the various pieces of the AM puzzle in order to enable professionals to see the bigger picture, inform their practices, and encourage further interdisciplinary research. The book is inspired by the now-classic *The Remembered Self: Emotion and Memory in Personality* written by Jefferson A. Singer and Peter Salovey (1993), which represented an important development in the area with its combination of social, clinical, and personality theories in discussing the relevance of memory for the self and psychotherapy. Our book also supplements the work initiated by Lusia in her 2009 edited book *Imagery and the Threatened Self: Perspectives on Mental Imagery and the Self in Cognitive Therapy*, which was arguably the first book to specifically link negative self-representations to distressing mental images in psychological disorders. The book is primarily aimed at clinicians and clinical trainees working with patients who experience difficulties related to adverse AMs; psychology postgraduate students; and researchers investigating AM and associated mental imagery, personality and the self, adverse AMs and imagery in psychological disorders, and the memory-self relationship in CBT.

The book has six chapters. Chapter 1 provides an overview of AM, its functions, and the factors that affect the ways in which individuals use their AMs in daily life. Chapter 2 explores the memory-self relationship in more depth. It focuses primarily on the role that AM and individuals' attempts to make sense of their experiences play in the development of a coherent sense of self over time. Chapter 3, on the other hand, focuses on the *immediate* impact of the retrieval of AMs on the self. Chapter 4 explores the implications of the memory-self relationship for psychological well-being. It focuses on the role that AMs and memory-related intrusive images play in psychopathology as they affect individuals' self-perceptions, emotions, and behaviour. Chapter 5 discusses the implications of the memory-self relationship for CBT. It focuses particularly on cognitive-behavioural interventions targeting adverse AMs and intrusive images and proposes a model for understanding mechanisms of change in these interventions. Finally, Chapter 6 reflects on the literature presented in the previous chapters and identifies ongoing debates and issues. The main goal of this chapter – like that of the whole book – is to highlight the ways in which different areas of psychology can contribute to each other in order to obtain a holistic perspective of AM and to develop more effective therapeutic interventions.

References

Baumeister, R. F. (1987). How the self became a problem: A psychological review of historical research. *Journal of Personality and Social Psychology, 52*(1), 163–176.

Bloch, D. (2007). *Aristotle on memory and recollection: Text, translation, interpretation, and reception in western scholasticism.* Leiden, The Netherlands: Brill.

Nelson, K. (2003). Self and social functions: Individual autobiographical memory and collective narrative. *Memory, 11*(2), 125–136.

Oppenheim, M. (2016, April 5). Sir Ian McKellen returns advance rumoured to be worth £1 million for his memoirs due to painful memories. *The Independent.* Retrieved from www.independent.co.uk

Ricoeur, P. (2004). *Memory, history, forgetting.* Chicago, IL: University of Chicago Press.

Santos, H. C., Varnum, M. E. W., & Grossmann, I. (2017). Global increases in individualism. *Psychological Science, 28*(9), 1228–1239.

Singer, J. A., & Salovey, P. (1993). *The remembered self: Emotion and memory in personality.* New York, NY: The Free Press.

Stopa, L. (Ed.) (2009). *Imagery and the threatened self: Perspectives on mental imagery and the self in cognitive therapy.* London, England: Routledge.

1 Introduction to autobiographical memory and its functions

What is autobiographical memory?

Autobiographical memories (AMs) are memories of events that happened in a specific time and place in one's personal past (Nelson, 2003; Nelson & Fivush, 2004). They are personally meaningful and are typically characterised by *autonoesis*, a sense of the self mentally travelling in time and re-experiencing the event (Tulving, 1985, 2002). Memories such as the first day of primary school, seeing one's child or a baby sibling for the first time, graduating from university, family gatherings, and failed attempts to attain career goals are all examples of meaningful AMs about which individuals would typically remember the context (e.g., time, place, other people present) and which they would recall from their own unique perspective.

In the last few decades, researchers have been systematically studying AMs. They have focused particularly on their functions, attempting to answer the questions: what do AMs actually do? How do individuals use them in their daily life? Is this use deliberate or unconscious? Is it adaptive or can it also lead to maladaptive outcomes? Understanding memory functions is crucial to understanding the relationship between AM and the self, as well as the implications of this relationship for psychopathology and clinical interventions. This chapter, therefore, focuses on the key functions of AM and the various ways in which different individuals rely on these functions.

Main functions of autobiographical memory

To date, memory researchers (e.g., Bluck, 2003; Bluck & Alea, 2002; Bluck, Alea, Habermas, & Rubin, 2005; Pillemer, 1992) have identified and investigated three key functions of AM: directive, self, and social. Below is a description of each function.

Directive function. This function refers to the role of AMs in guiding behaviour, cognition, and emotion (Pillemer, 2003). Individuals may use past experiences and the lessons learnt from them to solve problems, make decisions, plan future behaviour, motivate themselves, manage their emotions, make sense of their experiences, and update their view of themselves or their life (Bluck & Alea, 2002; Bluck et al., 2005; Pillemer, 2003). Therefore, AMs enable individuals to function on a daily basis as they navigate their environments and adapt to them. In fact, Pillemer (2003) argues that using AMs for directive purposes has evolutionary value: by guiding behaviour, AMs can facilitate survival. They can do this on a conscious level or by operating outside conscious awareness. When faced with a challenging problem, for example, individuals may deliberately recall experiences relevant to this problem that can help them solve it. After a traumatic experience such as an accident, they may try to protect themselves by deliberately avoiding situations or stimuli that remind them of this accident or that they believe could cause another one. In a threatening situation, however, they may also respond automatically (e.g., by fleeing) instead of stopping to recall similar past circumstances and then deciding what to do. According to Pillemer, in threatening situations it is essential to activate past AMs which can deliver their directives into consciousness quickly. Reminiscence and effortful memory activities may be time consuming and prevent a quick response in such situations.

Self function. This function concerns the role of AM in the development and maintenance of a continuous, coherent, and ideally positive sense of self (Bluck, 2003; Bluck et al., 2005; Conway & Pleydell-Pearce, 2000; Conway, Singer, & Tagini, 2004; Demiray & Janssen, 2015; Nelson, 2003; Wilson & Ross, 2003). Individuals use their AMs to construct a *life story* or *narrative identity* – an evolving story about how their past, present, and future selves are part of a single, integrated person (McAdams, 2001, 2008, 2015; Singer, 2004). As we will see in Chapters 2 and 4, this story gives them a sense of coherence, meaning, and direction in life and is crucial for psychological well-being (McAdams, 2015; McAdams & McLean, 2013). To illustrate, take the example of a person coming from a low-socioeconomic-status family who achieves upward social mobility through university education and a high-status occupation. This person has to reconcile their "working class" and "middle class" identities while navigating their different environments (e.g., working class family settings and relationships and diverse professional contexts). If they have emigrated, they also have to reconcile their national identity with their identity as a migrant who may have become acculturated to their country of residence. This is in addition to the other roles and identities they need to reconcile, for example as daughter/son, sibling, grandchild, aunt/uncle, niece/nephew, friend, partner, and so on. For every role or identity, they will have specific AMs from which they have learnt lessons or drawn conclusions about themselves. In order to achieve a holistic understanding of who they are, why they are this way, and what direction they need to take in the future, they need to process the different AMs associated with the complex identities and link them together in order to create a coherent story about themselves.

The relationship between AMs and the self is so strong that individuals may maintain a relatively stable and accurate sense of self even when they have suffered partial memory loss due to organic syndromes such as Alzheimer's disease (see Eustache, Viard, & Desgranges, 2016; Rathbone, Moulin, & Conway, 2009) or find it difficult to retrieve specific memories (see Klein, Cosmides, Costabile, & Mei, 2002). This relationship is bidirectional (see Wilson & Ross, 2003). On the one hand, the past lays the foundations on which individuals construct the self by providing the memories used to build their narrative identity. On the other hand, the self and its goals may affect the way in which they construct and recall their past. Individuals can, for example, reappraise their AMs in terms of relevance or positive/negative emotional valence to make them fit the narrative they have created about themselves. If their narrative features them as survivors who always succeed against all odds, they may minimise their failures and emphasise or feel psychologically closer to their achievements. If their narrative features them as incompetent and inept, they may discount their successes.

Social function. This function is related to the use of AM in developing and nurturing interpersonal relationships (Bluck et al., 2005). As Nelson (2003) puts it, nowadays it is not sufficient to have a story about one's life: this story also needs to be presented effectively to others. This presentation and sharing of personal experiences or narratives helps individuals appear credible and genuine, get to know each other on a deeper level, empathise with others or elicit empathy from them, and help each other with information and advice (Alea & Bluck, 2003; Bluck et al., 2005). For example, if a person explains that their difficulty in trusting people is partly due to negative experiences of being lied to or betrayed, this may help the other person understand him/her better and potentially empathise. It may also encourage the listener to share their own experiences of disappointment or betrayal. Ultimately, such exchanges may create a sense of intimacy which may be particularly important if the lack of trust had previously created problems in this relationship.

Additional functions of autobiographical memory

The directive, self, and social functions of AM to date have been investigated primarily using the questionnaire Thinking About Life Experiences (TALE; Bluck et al., 2005) and its revised version (TALE-R; Bluck & Alea, 2011). The items in these questionnaires begin with the stem *"I think back over or talk about my life or certain periods of my life..."* and include statements such as *"when I need to make a life choice and I am uncertain which path to take," "when I want to understand how I have changed from who I was before,"* and *"when I hope to also find out what another person is like."* Participants indicate how often they use their past for each function. Although the TALE is based on the existing literature on memory functions, some evidence suggests that it is not exhaustive. Using his Reminiscence Functions Scale (RFS), which has a similar structure to the TALE, Webster (1993) has identified the use of reminiscence for problem solving, identity purposes, conversation, boredom reduction, intimacy maintenance, death preparation (reviewing one's life in preparation for death and having a sense of completion or achievement), teaching/informing others, and revival of bitterness (reminiscence of unjust experiences). As Bluck and Alea (2002) point out, however, there are overlaps between the TALE and RFS categories. According to these authors, death preparation and identity correspond to the self function; problem solving corresponds to the directive function; and conversation, intimacy maintenance, and teaching/informing correspond to the social function.

Harris, Rasmussen, and Berntsen (2014) reached a similar conclusion to Bluck and Alea's (2002). These authors combined the TALE-R with the RFS and examined the convergence/divergence of the two scales. They identified four functions of AM: reflective, social, ruminative, and generative. The reflective function seemed to represent an overlap between the self and directive functions identified by previous research. It involved using self-focused attention to reflect about the self, while also managing behaviour and regulating emotions. The social function involved engaging in conversations and social bonding. The ruminative function was related to the use of AM to focus attention on the self and dwell primarily on losses and threats. Finally, the generative function involved using AM to teach or inform others and feel a sense of achievement while facing one's mortality. This last function resonates with evidence that intergenerational stories (stories about one's past that are shared with younger family members, usually by parents or grandparents) may help adults achieve generativity (positive legacy by caring for and promoting the well-being and success of the younger generations) in midlife (see Merrill & Fivush, 2016).

Based on their findings, Harris and colleagues (2014) suggest that AM may play functions other than the ones captured by existing measures. One of the examples they present is that of emotion regulation, which in the TALE is associated primarily with the directive function but is not included in the TALE-R. Other examples include non-conscious uses of AM that are not captured by measures such as the TALE, which explicitly instructs participants to indicate when they think about their past and thus focuses on memory functions within conscious awareness. Clearly, further research and new measures are needed to obtain a more thorough understanding of how individuals use AMs in their daily life.

Autobiographical memory functions and context

From the account of memory functions presented earlier, it may seem as if these functions are neatly separated from each other or as if individual memories serve only one function. In reality, memory functions overlap and are context dependent (Bluck, 2003, 2017; Bluck & Alea, 2002). First, individuals can use the same AM for different purposes at different times. Someone can remember graduating top of their class in order to develop or strengthen a view of themselves as smart and hardworking (self function). They can use the same memory to motivate themselves when dealing with a task that seems overwhelming (directive function). They can also share this memory with others in order to provide a glimpse into who they are and build intimacy (social function). They can use the memory for these purposes at the same time or in different moments. Second, they may use this memory depending on the context. In a social context, for example, how they use the memory may depend on who the listener is and how responsive he/she is. They may provide more detail and use their AMs for social functions when talking to others who are similar to them, who are responsive during the conversation (e.g., demonstrate interest through body language or questions), and with whom they are more familiar and have a long relationship (see Alea & Bluck, 2003).

Autobiographical memory functions and characteristics

Memory characteristics can also affect how individuals use their past experiences. Positive AMs, for example, may be more likely to serve self and social functions than negative AMs (McLean & Lilgendahl, 2008; Rasmussen & Berntsen, 2009; Thorne & McLean, 2003), potentially because they help preserve a positive view of the self and are shared more frequently (e.g., Baker-Ward, Eaton, & Banks, 2005; Byrne, Hyman, & Scott, 2001). Negative AMs, on the other hand, may be more likely than positive ones to serve directive functions (Alea, Arneaud, & Ali, 2013). This may have an evolutionary advantage as lessons learnt from past failures may help avoid similar mistakes in the future (Pillemer, 2003).

Valence, however, is not the only memory characteristic affecting the use of AMs. The type of memory may also play a role. Demiray and Freund (2015) found that the directive function was served to a similar extent by positive and negative flashbulb memories (vivid AMs in which individuals first learnt about a relevant and emotional event, for example the results of the 2016 Brexit referendum or the United States presidential election). Rasmussen and Berntsen (2009) argue that involuntary memories (i.e., memories that arise spontaneously) may be particularly likely to serve self-continuity and directive functions when individuals encounter novel situations or engage in problem solving. This may happen because their activation requires less cognitive control than voluntary memories.

Autobiographical memory functions and individual differences

In addition to the immediate context and memory characteristics, the use of AMs may also be influenced by individual characteristics. To date, the evidence on this phenomenon is patchy; we know more about some characteristics than others. Nevertheless, it is slowly growing and providing a better insight into the relevance of AMs. Some of the characteristics that researchers have identified so far are culture, age, gender, personality attributes, and emotional state or psychological well-being.

Culture. The existing literature acknowledges that what we remember and how we remember it is crucial to how we define ourselves (Bluck & Habermas, 2000; McLean, Pasupathi, & Pals, 2007). This *what* and *how*, however, does not develop or manifest itself in a vacuum. AM is embedded in the individual's social and cultural context and is thus moulded by it (see Alea & Wang, 2015; Nelson & Fivush, 2004; Wang & Brockmeier, 2002). By growing up and living in a certain environment, we develop a cultural understanding of the self that is thought to affect the nature, accessibility, and function of AM (Wang, 2013).

Nelson and Fivush's (2004) sociocultural developmental theory of the emergence of AM explains how this process occurs beginning from the pre-school years (around age 3.5 years in Western countries), influenced by factors such as understanding of time, the development of the theory of mind and representation of the self, and the environment. According to this theory, the environment is crucial. Factors such as the frequency with which pre-school children talk with their caregivers about past or future experiences, the details they focus on in these conversations, and the caregivers' involvement (e.g., elaboration or questions provided) may shape children's understanding of their own and others' mental states, their view of themselves relative to others, and the way in which they organise and narrate their AMs (Fivush, 2011; Merrill & Fivush, 2016; Nelson & Fivush, 2004). Greater elaboration (e.g., requests to reflect and elaborate on thoughts or emotions experienced during an event) and a more complex narrative style on the part of the caregivers may enable children to recall, rehearse, and recount their experiences in a detailed, coherent manner. This may then contribute to the development of an enduring sense of self which reconciles past and present self-representations. In a similar manner, caregivers may encourage the development of a view of the self as independent (e.g., by emphasising the child's individuality, goals, desires, and emotions in memory conversations) or as embedded in one's social group (e.g., by emphasising social interactions). They may thus promote a construal of the self (independent vs interdependent) that is in line with Markus and Kitayama's (1991, 2010) account of differences between Western and non-Western cultures.

Evidence supports the main arguments of Nelson and Fivush's (2004) theory. It suggests that the way in which AMs are formed, narrated, and used in a particular culture may be affected by factors such as economic development (Alea, Bluck, & Ali, 2015), geographical location (Sahin-Acar & Leichtman, 2015), oral history tradition (Nile & Van Bergen, 2015; Reese & Neha, 2015), cultural practices encouraging or discouraging AM recall and sharing (see Bluck, 2015), the value that cultures place on memories' relevance for the self, and their view of the self as autonomous or interdependent (Wang & Brockmeier, 2002). In Western countries, individuals are more likely to report memories that are specific and self-focused than individuals in more collectivistic (e.g., East Asian) countries, whose memories tend to be less specific and more socially oriented (e.g., Han, Leichtman, & Wang, 1998; Wang, 2004; Wang & Conway, 2004). These differences seem to be related to cultural differences in mothers' conversational or reminiscing styles. Schröder, Kärtner, and Keller (2015) found differences between German and Indian mothers in terms of how they recounted stories of their first year of life to their children (e.g., level of elaboration and portrayal of the child as unique or not). Similarly, Sahin-Acar and Leichtman (2015) found that mothers in the United States (US) were more elaborative in memory conversations than Eastern Turkish mothers, who tend to be more traditional and encourage the development of less specific AMs in their children. Western Turkish mothers, who arguably live in a more progressive environment than their counterparts in Eastern Turkey, fell somewhere in between the US and Eastern Turkish mothers. This and other findings (e.g., Aviezer, Sher-Censor, & Stein-Lahad, 2017; Göz, Çeven, & Tekcan, 2017) suggest that cultural variations in caregiver-child memory conversations and AM content (e.g., level of detail and involvement of others) may exist even within the same culture.

In addition to AM content and self-construals, culture may also influence the ways in which individuals use their AMs. Evidence suggests that the self, social, and directive functions of AM are universal (Alea & Wang, 2015). It seems, however, that individuals' beliefs about memory functions and the extent to which they use AMs for specific purposes varies among cultures. For example, individuals from Trinidad (Alea et al., 2015) and Japan (Maki, Kawasaki, Demiray, & Janssen, 2015) use AMs less frequently for self and social functions than individuals in the US. This may be because interdependent cultures have practices that promote a strong sense of social identity and social bonding, so their members do not need to rely as much on AMs (Alea & Wang, 2015; Liao, Bluck, Alea, & Cheng, 2016; Wang, 2013). In these cultures, AM may be used more for other purposes. In Asian cultures, it may be valued more for didactic and directive purposes (see Wang, 2013; Wang, Koh, Song, & Hou, 2015). Taiwanese emerging adults may use AMs more for self purposes because they live in a culture that is shifting from collectivism to individualism but is not yet supportive of the forging of a unique identity (Liao et al., 2016). Indigenous Australians may be more likely than non-Indigenous ones to use AMs in order to teach and inform others, potentially because they have a strong oral tradition and this use of AMs helps them preserve and transmit their cultural values (Nile & Van Bergen, 2015). As these examples suggest, AM functions are used when needed the most (Bluck, Alea, & Demiray, 2010).

Age. Some evidence suggests that the use of AMs can vary during the life course, even though findings are not always consistent. Bluck and Alea (2009) found that young and older adults did not differ in the extent to which they used AM for social bonding. Other researchers, however, suggest that young adults may be more likely than older adults to use AMs for self, social, and directive functions, potentially because they face key developmental tasks that involve establishing an identity, developing interpersonal relationships, and making important life decisions (Alea et al., 2015; Bluck & Alea, 2008; McLean & Lilgendahl, 2008; Wolf & Zimprich, 2015). Yet more research suggests that, even though older adults use AM for self-related purposes just like young adults, they may do so for different reasons, for example for death preparation rather than identity construction (Webster & McCall, 1999). In fact, older adults may be more likely than young adults to use AMs (especially positive ones) for death preparation and in order to teach or inform others (McLean & Lilgendahl, 2008; Nile & Van Bergen, 2015; Webster & McCall, 1999). The use of AMs in older age, however, may vary. O'Rourke, King, and Cappeliez (2017), for example, found that in older age there is temporal stability of the self and directive functions but temporal variability of the social function. According to these authors, this may be due to the fact that the social function depends on individuals' emotional states and opportunities for sharing AMs with others.

Gender. Research suggests that women may be more likely to reminisce than men, but the evidence on gender differences in the functional uses of AM is inconsistent (e.g., Alea et al., 2015; Harris et al., 2014; Maki et al., 2015). What current evidence shows, however, is that parents (especially mothers) can be more elaborative and evaluative in memory conversations with their daughters than with their sons and that sometimes this translates into females recalling and describing more detailed and more emotionally intense memories than males (Fivush, Berlin, McDermott, Mennuti-Washburn, & Cassidy, 2003; Grysman, Merrill, & Fivush, 2017; Pillemer, Wink, DiDonato, & Sanborn, 2003; Reese & Fivush, 1993; Reese & Neha, 2015).

Personality attributes. Preliminary evidence suggests that personality characteristics can also affect individuals' use of their AMs. This evidence is limited and needs replication, so it should be treated with caution. Nevertheless, it provides interesting insights into four characteristics: (1) conscientiousness (personality factor associated with efficiency, self-discipline, organisation, and achievement striving); (2) openness to experience (personality factor associated with curiosity, wide interests, unconventional values, and excitability) (John & Srivastava, 1999); (3) self-concept clarity (the extent to which individuals' self-concept is clear, consistent, and stable over time) (Campbell et al., 1996); and (4) self-esteem (individuals' global evaluation of their self-worth) (Rosenberg, 1965).

To date, research has shown that individuals who score high in conscientiousness and individuals who score low in self-concept clarity may be more likely to use their AMs in order to maintain self-continuity

(Bluck & Alea, 2008; Liao et al., 2016). Being particularly dutiful and self-disciplined or being unclear about one's self-concept, therefore, may encourage individuals to rely on AMs in order to enhance their view of the self as consistent and stable over time. Individuals who score high in self-esteem, on the other hand, may be more likely to rehearse and feel psychologically closer to positive AMs (i.e., perceive them as temporally closer and more connected to their present self) and thus use these AMs to enhance their view of themselves (Demiray & Janssen, 2015). When it comes to openness to experience, researchers have found that it is positively associated with the extent to which individuals remember their past and perceive this as beneficial (Rasmussen & Berntsen, 2010). Furthermore, openness may be related to the use of AM for self and directive functions, potentially because individuals who are high in openness could be more willing to explore and use their AMs strategically (Rasmussen & Berntsen, 2010).

Psychological well-being. Finally, some research indicates that the use of AMs may be affected by individuals' emotional state or overall psychological well-being. Grace, Dewhirst, and Anderson (2016) suggest that depression levels may be positively correlated with the frequency of recalling AMs for self-continuity functions. According to these authors, this may be due to rumination, self-focused attention, and a wish to "repair" one's self-concept. Reminiscence, however, may not necessarily achieve its aim in dysphoric or depressed individuals. In fact, Grace and colleagues found that individuals with higher levels of depressive symptoms were less likely to find talking about their past experiences useful or beneficial. For these individuals, therefore, recalling or sharing AMs may not necessarily lead to a perception of the self as continuous and consistent. Instead, it may be counterproductive and help maintain low mood.

Conclusion

As the literature reviewed in this chapter suggests, AM plays a crucial role in our daily lives. It shapes how we see ourselves and others; how we form and maintain interpersonal relationships; and how we think, feel, and behave. As such, it may contribute to healthy functioning by leading to a sense of purpose and communion (i.e., purpose in life, personal growth, generativity feelings), as well as positive relationships with others (Waters, 2014). The way in which AM affects us depends on how we use and narrate it, which in turn may depend on its characteristics, the context we find ourselves in, and our own unique attributes.

As discussed in this chapter, AMs can be used deliberately to deal with present circumstances or may operate outside of conscious awareness. Regardless of whether the process is conscious or not, its outcomes can be either positive or negative. Processing a negative experience such as being publicly humiliated and linking it to other similar experiences may contribute to a view of the self as flawed or inadequate. Sharing a past experience with another person may backfire and put an end to a relationship instead of strengthening it. Using a past experience to manage one's emotions or respond to a situation may not always be helpful, either. For example, compulsively washing hands and disinfecting personal objects because in the past this has reduced the anxiety triggered by contamination fears may be temporarily helpful but maintain these fears in the long run. The negative consequences of AM will be described in greater detail in Chapters 3 and 4. For now, however, it is important to obtain a better understanding of the memory-self relationship. This is the aim of Chapter 2.

References

Alea, N., Arneaud, M. J., & Ali, S. (2013). The quality of self, social, and directive memories: Are there adult age group differences? *International Journal of Behavioral Development, 37*, 395–406.

Alea, N. & Bluck, S. (2003). Why are you telling me that? A conceptual model of the social function of autobiographical memory. *Memory, 11*(2), 165–178.

Alea, N., Bluck, S., & Ali, S. (2015). Function in context: Why American and Trinidadian young and older adults remember the personal past. *Memory, 23*(1), 55–68.

Alea, N. & Wang, Q. (2015). Going global: The functions of autobiographical memory in cultural context. *Memory, 23*(1), 1–10.

Aviezer, O., Sher-Censor, E., & Stein-Lahad, T. (2017). Earliest memories in Israeli kibbutz upbringing: It is parental engagement that makes a difference. *Memory, 25*(10), 1375–1389.

Baker-Ward, L. E., Eaton, K. L., & Banks, J. B. (2005). Young soccer players' reports of a tournament win or loss: Different emotions, different narratives. *Journal of Cognition and Development, 6*, 507–527.

Bluck, S. (2003). Autobiographical memory: Exploring its functions in everyday life. *Memory, 11*(2), 113–123.

Bluck, S. (2015). Going global: Functions of autobiographical remembering world tour. *Memory, 23*(1), 111–118.

Bluck, S. (2017). Remember and review or forget and let go? Views from a functional approach to autobiographical memory. *The International Journal of Reminiscence and Life Review, 4*(1), 3–7.

Bluck, S. & Alea, N. (2002). Exploring the functions of autobiographical memory: Why do I remember the autumn? In J. D. Webster & B. K. Haight

(Eds.), *Critical advances in reminiscence: From theory to application* (pp. 61–75). New York, NY: Springer.

Bluck, S. & Alea, N. (2008). Remembering being me: The self-continuity function of autobiographical memory in younger and older adults. In F. Sani (Ed.), *Self-continuity: Individual and collective perspectives* (pp. 55–70). New York, NY: Psychology Press.

Bluck, S. & Alea, N. (2009). Thinking and talking about the past: Why remember? *Applied Cognitive Psychology, 23*(8), 1089–1104.

Bluck, S. & Alea, N. (2011). Crafting the TALE: Construction of a measure to assess the functions of autobiographical remembering. *Memory, 19*(5), 470–486.

Bluck, S., Alea, N., & Demiray, B. (2010). You get what you need: The psychosocial functions of remembering. In J. H. Mace (Ed.), *The act of remembering: Toward an understanding of how we recall the past* (pp. 284–307). Malden, MA: Wiley-Blackwell.

Bluck, S., Alea, N., Habermas, T., & Rubin, D. C. (2005). A tale of three functions: The self-reported uses of autobiographical memory. *Social Cognition, 23*(1), 91–117.

Bluck, S. & Habermas, T. (2000). The life story schema. *Motivation and Emotion, 24*(2), 121–147.

Byrne, C. A., Hyman, I. E., & Scott, K. L. (2001). Comparisons of memories for traumatic events and other experiences. *Applied Cognitive Psychology, 15*, 119–133.

Campbell, J. D., Trapnell, P. D., Heine, S. J., Katz, I. M., Lavallee, L. F., & Lehman, D. R. (1996). Self-concept clarity: Measurement, personality correlates, and cultural boundaries. *Journal of Personality and Social Psychology, 70*(1), 141–156.

Conway, M. A., & Pleydell-Pearce, C. W. (2000). The construction of autobiographical memories in the self-memory system. *Psychological Review, 107*(2), 261–288.

Conway, M. A., Singer, J. A., & Tagini, A. (2004). The self and autobiographical memory: Correspondence and coherence. *Social Cognition, 22*(5), 491–529.

Demiray, B. & Freund, A. M. (2015). Michael Jackson, Bin Laden and I: Functions of positive and negative, public and private flashbulb memories. *Memory, 23*(4), 487–506.

Demiray, B. & Janssen, S. M. (2015). The self-enhancement function of autobiographical memory. *Applied Cognitive Psychology, 29*(1), 49–60.

Eustache, F., Viard, A., & Desgranges, B. (2016). The MNESIS model: Memory systems and processes, identity and future thinking. *Neuropsychologia, 87*, 96–109.

Fivush, R. (2011). The development of autobiographical memory. In S. T. Fiske, D. L. Schacter, & S. E. Taylor (Eds.), *Annual review of psychology* (Vol. 62, pp. 550–582). Palo Alto, CA: Annual Reviews.

Fivush, R., Berlin, L., Sales, J. D., Mennuti-Washburn, J., & Cassidy, J. (2003). Functions of parent-child reminiscing about emotionally negative events. *Memory, 11*, 179–192.

Göz, İ., Çeven, Z. İ., & Tekcan, A. İ. (2017). Urban-rural differences in children's earliest memories. *Memory, 25*(2), 214–219.

Grace, L., Dewhurst, S. A., & Anderson, R. J. (2016). A dysphoric's TALE: The relationship between the self-reported functions of autobiographical memory and symptoms of depression. *Memory, 24*(9), 1173–1181.

Grysman, A., Merrill, N., & Fivush, R. (2017). Emotion, gender, and gender typical identity in autobiographical memory. *Memory, 25*(3), 289–297.

Han, J. J., Leichtman, M. D., & Wang, Q. (1998). Autobiographical memory in Korean, Chinese, and American children. *Developmental Psychology, 34*, 701–713.

Harris, C. B., Rasmussen, A. S., & Berntsen, D. (2014). The functions of autobiographical memory: An integrative approach. *Memory, 22*(5), 559–581.

John, O. P. & Srivastava, S. (1999). The Big-Five trait taxonomy: History, measurement, and theoretical perspectives. In L. A. Pervin & O. P. John (Eds.), *Handbook of personality: Theory and research* (Vol. 2, pp. 102–138). New York, NY: Guilford Press.

Klein, S. B., Cosmides, L., Costabile, K. A., & Mei, L. (2002). Is there something special about the self? A neuropsychological case study. *Journal of Research in Personality, 36*, 490–506.

Liao, H.-W., Bluck, S., Alea, N., & Cheng, C.-L. (2016). Functions of autobiographical memory in Taiwanese and American emerging adults. *Memory, 24*(4), 423–436.

Maki, Y., Kawasaki, Y., Demiray, B., & Janssen, S. M. J. (2015). Autobiographical memory functions in young Japanese men and women. *Memory, 23*(1), 11–24.

Markus, H. R. & Kitayama, S. (1991). Culture and the self: Implications for cognition, emotion, and motivation. *Psychological Review, 98*(2), 224–253.

Markus, H. R. & Kitayama, S. (2010). Cultures and selves: A cycle of mutual constitution. *Perspectives on Psychological Science, 5*(4), 420–430.

McAdams, D. P. (2001). The psychology of life stories. *Review of General Psychology, 5*(2), 100–122.

McAdams, D. P. (2008). Personal narratives and the life story. In O. P. John, R. W. Robins, & L. A. Pervin (Eds.), *Handbook of personality: Theory and research (3rd ed.)* (pp. 242–262). New York, NY: Guilford Press.

McAdams, D. P. (2015). *The art and science of personality development.* New York, NY: Guilford Press.

McAdams, D. P. & McLean, K. C. (2013). Narrative identity. *Current Directions in Psychological Science, 22*(3), 233–238.

McLean, K. C. & Lilgendahl, J. (2008). Why recall our highs and lows: Relations between memory functions, age, and well-being. *Memory, 16*(7), 751–762.

McLean, K. C., Pasupathi, M., & Pals, J. L. (2007). Selves creating stories creating selves: A process model of narrative self development in adolescence and adulthood. *Personality and Social Psychology Review, 11*, 262–278.

Merrill, N. & Fivush, R. (2016). Intergenerational narratives and identity across development. *Development Review, 40*, 72–92.

Nelson, K. (2003). Self and social functions: Individual autobiographical memory and collective narrative. *Memory, 11*(2), 125–136.

Nelson, K. & Fivush, R. (2004). The emergence of autobiographical memory: A social cultural developmental theory. *Psychological Review, 111*(2), 486–511.

Nile, E. & Van Bergen, P. (2015). Not all semantics: Similarities and differences in reminiscing function and content between Indigenous and non-Indigenous Australians. *Memory, 23*(1), 83–98.

O'Rourke, N., King, D. B., & Cappeliez, P. (2017). Reminiscence functions over time: Consistency of self functions and variation of prosocial functions. *Memory, 25*(3), 403–411.

Pillemer, D. B. (1992). Remembering personal circumstances: A functional analysis. In E. Winograd & U. Neisser (Eds.), *Affect and accuracy in recall: Studies of "flashbulb" memories* (pp. 236–264). New York, NY: Cambridge University Press.

Pillemer, D. (2003). Directive functions of autobiographical memory: The guiding power of the specific episode. *Memory, 11*(2), 193–202.

Pillemer, D., Wink, P., DiDonato, T., & Sanborn, R. (2003). Gender differences in autobiographical memory styles of older adults. *Memory, 11*, 525–532.

Rasmussen, A. S. & Berntsen, D. (2009). The possible functions of involuntary autobiographical memories. *Applied Cognitive Psychology, 23*(8), 1137–1152.

Rasmussen, A. S. & Berntsen, D. (2010). Personality traits and autobiographical memory: Openness is positively related to the experience and usage of recollections. *Memory, 18*(7), 774–786.

Rathbone, C. J., Moulin, C. J. A., & Conway, M. A. (2009). Autobiographical memory and amnesia: Using conceptual knowledge to ground the self. *Neurocase, 15*(5), 405–418.

Reese, E. & Fivush, R. (1993). Parental styles of talking about the past. *Developmental Psychology, 29*, 596–606.

Reese, E. & Neha, T. (2015). Let's kōrero (talk): The practice and functions of reminiscing among mothers and children in Māori families. *Memory, 23*(1), 99–110.

Rosenberg, M. (1965). *Society and the adolescent self-image.* Princeton, NJ: Princeton University.

Sahin-Acar, B. & Leichtman, M. D. (2015). Mother-child memory conversations and self-construal in Eastern Turkey, Western Turkey and the USA. *Memory, 23*(1), 69–82.

Schröder, L., Kärtner, J., & Keller, H. (2015). Telling a "baby story": Mothers narrating their pre-schoolers' past across two cultural contexts. *Memory, 23*(1), 39–54.

Singer, J. A. (2004). Narrative identity and meaning-making across the adult span: An introduction. *Journal of Personality, 72*, 437–459.

Thorne, A. & McLean, K. C. (2003). Gendered reminiscence practices and self-definition in late adolescence. *Sex Roles, 46*, 261–271.

Tulving, E. (1985). Memory and consciousness. *Canadian Psychology/ Psychologie Canadienne, 26*(1), 1–12.

Tulving, E. (2002). Episodic memory: From mind to brain. *Annual Review of Psychology, 53*(1), 1–25.

Wang, Q. (2004). The emergence of cultural self-constructs: Autobiographical memory and self-description in European, American and Chinese children. *Developmental Psychology, 40*, 3–15.

Wang, Q. (2013). *The autobiographical self in time and culture.* New York, NY: Oxford University Press.

Wang, Q. & Brockmeier, J. (2002). Autobiographical remembering as cultural practice: Understanding the interplay between memory, self and culture. *Culture & Psychology, 8*(1), 45–64.

Wang, Q. & Conway, M. A. (2004). The stories we keep: Autobiographical memory in American and Chinese middle-aged adults. *Journal of Personality, 72*(5), 911–938.

Wang, Q., Koh, J. B. K., Song, Q., & Hou, Y. (2015). Knowledge of memory functions in European and Asian American adults and children: The relation to autobiographical memory. *Memory, 23*(1), 25–38.

Waters, T. E. A. (2014). Relations between the functions of autobiographical memory and psychological wellbeing. *Memory, 22*(3), 265–275.

Webster, J. D. (1993). Construction and validation of the Reminiscence Functions Scale. *Journal of Gerontology: Psychological Sciences, 48*(5), 256–262.

Webster, J. D. & McCall, M. (1999). Reminiscence functions across adulthood: A replication and extension. *Journal of Adult Development, 6*(1), 73–85.

Wilson, A. E. & Ross, M. (2003). The identity function of autobiographical memory: Time is on our side. *Memory, 11*(2), 137–149.

Wolf, T. & Zimprich, D. (2015). Differences in the use of autobiographical memory across the adult lifespan. *Memory, 23*(8), 1238–1254.

2 The journey from concrete experience to abstract self-knowledge: How autobiographical memory contributes to the development of the self

Introduction

The previous chapter reported that one of the key functions of autobiographical memory (AM) is the development and maintenance of a positive, coherent sense of self that is perceived by the individual as relatively stable over time. Based on the existing literature, we stated that individuals use their past experiences to develop an idea of who they are and to construct a narrative thread that links their past, present, and future selves. In the present chapter, we rely on the work of researchers like Dan P. McAdams, Jefferson A. Singer, Tilmann Habermas, Susan Bluck, and Kate C. McLean to explain *how* this passage from experience to memory to self happens. Our aim is not to provide a detailed account of the existing literature (McAdams has already done an excellent job with this in his 2015 book *The Art and Science of Personality Development*). Rather, we want to provide an overview of the process in order to illustrate how individuals make sense of their experiences and themselves. This can help us understand better the clinical literature on the adverse effects of negative or traumatic memories that will be discussed later on in this book. As Luke and Stopa (2009) argue, an understanding of negative self processes or distorted self-views in psychological disorders requires first and foremost an understanding of how the self develops and is maintained in healthy individuals.

To gain an overview of the memory-self relationship, we first clarify what we mean by *self*. We then move on to McAdams' life story model of personality development and related research, presenting the different ways in which individuals make sense of their experiences as they attempt to build a coherent sense of self. We also focus on the role that age and culture play in this process. Next, we discuss the role that emotions and goals play in determining which memories are retained in long-term memory. We conclude by describing the characteristics of the memories that help define the self.

What exactly is the self?

Before we take a closer look at the memory-self relationship, it is important to provide a definition of the self. As often happens in psychology, there is no universally accepted definition for this construct and the literature is generally inconsistent when it comes to the use of the terms *self*, *identity*, and *personality* (see Leary & Tangney, 2012). For example, the terms *self* and *identity* are sometimes used as synonymous (Swann & Bosson, 2010). At other times, identity is seen as individuals' general idea of who they are or is conceptualised primarily in terms of the roles and group memberships that make up this idea (see Oyserman, Elmore, & Smith, 2012). Personality, on the other hand, is sometimes discussed only in terms of personality traits (see Morf & Mischel, 2012; Syed, 2017).

In recent years, researchers have provided more comprehensive definitions of identity, personality, and the self. Perhaps the most comprehensive framework is that provided by McAdams (e.g., McAdams, 1996, 2015a; McAdams & Pals, 2006), who conceives of personality as a dynamic representation that delineates individuals' uniqueness; is embedded in their social and cultural context; and encompasses their dispositional traits (e.g., extraversion), characteristic adaptations such as personal goals and values, as well as the life story or narrative identity (i.e., their narrative of who they were, who they are, and who they may become). Based on William James' (1892) theory, the self is seen as an observing conscious agent (the *I*) and an observed *Me* which consists of what the *I* attributes to itself (see McAdams, 2013). It involves the narrative identity constructed by the *I* and other personality components or characteristics that the individual is aware of. This conceptualisation is in line with other recent definitions. For example, Morf and Mischel (2012) view the self as a psychosocial dynamic processing system which includes representations of the self (e.g., *"me as a daughter"*), beliefs about the self (e.g., *"I am not practical at all"*), traits, goals, positive and negative affect, values, and scripts for generating behaviours (e.g., steps to follow when entering the classroom to deliver a lecture). Conway, Singer, and Tagini (2004), on the other hand, see the stable sense of self (which they refer to as the *long-term self*) as consisting of individuals' autobiographical knowledge (conceptual knowledge about their past experiences and their understanding of the normative life in their culture) and their conceptual self (structure containing conceptual information about the self, for example about traits, values, and beliefs). Other researchers (e.g., Leary & Tangney, 2012; Markus & Kitayama, 2010) view the self as a set of psychological constructs and processes that enable individuals to focus on, think about, and regulate themselves (e.g., manage their emotions or behaviours) depending on the context they find themselves in.

As the above definitions suggest, the self is viewed as inextricably linked to memory. For this reason, in this chapter – and in the rest of the book – we use the term *self* to denote individuals' experience-based narratives regarding their past, present, and future; as well as their knowledge about themselves, including their self-beliefs, personality traits, goals, values, roles, and social identities. In order to explain its development, we rely on the life story model of personality development (e.g., McAdams, 2015a) and the work of researchers who have built on it. Our rationale for using this model is that it is supported by significant empirical evidence and is currently considered as the state of the art in personality psychology (see Syed, 2017). Furthermore, we believe that this model and the research it has inspired fit very well with our understanding of psychological disorders linked to adverse AMs and intrusive mental images, which will be discussed in Chapters 4 and 5. Following is an overview of the model.

The life story model of personality development

McAdams (1995, 2001, 2008, 2013, 2015a, 2015b) proposes that personality consists of three related layers that develop at different stages in the lifespan. The first layer, which is dominant in infancy, involves the child as a *social actor* whose behaviour is primarily influenced by dispositional traits or propensities (e.g., extraversion) and the social roles that they need to play in different contexts. The second layer becomes prominent in middle childhood (around ages 5–7) and involves children as *motivated agents* who have an agenda. In this stage, children develop values, coping strategies, hopes and fears, skills, and life goals which begin to shape their behaviour and orient them towards the future. They come to consciously understand themselves in terms of their goals and become better able to formulate and enact plans for achieving these goals. They also start developing more complex representations of themselves and others based on their own observations and on others' feedback. Although they can provide descriptions of themselves and others, they are not normally able to reason about why they or others are who they are. They become effective at doing this in late adolescence and early adulthood, when the third layer of personality – the life story – starts to develop. During this stage, as Erikson (1963) theorises, young people face the challenge of developing an identity and experience social pressure to do so. They thus become *autobiographical authors* who try to give themselves an identity by constructing complex narratives about themselves and their life that include, for example, plots, settings, scenes characterised by imagery, characters or different representations of the self, conflicts, and themes (goal-directed sequences that they pursue in the narrative) (McAdams, 1985, 1995, 2015a, 2015b). The stories that they construct and share with their growing social networks are meaningful, are constantly edited and reinterpreted, and help them explain what has happened to them in the past and why, how they have developed and changed over time, and who they may become in the future (McAdams, 2001, 2013, 2015a, 2015b; McAdams & McLean, 2013; McLean, Pasupathi, & Pals, 2007).

According to Singer and Salovey (1993, p. 70), "the stories that individuals tell about their own lives are the life blood of personality." They help us understand what is unique about a person: individuals may have the same traits and goals and go through the same experiences, but they are likely to construct unique stories about these experiences and about themselves (Singer & Blagov, 2004; Syed, 2017). In the life story model, these stories constitute individuals' narrative identity, which comprises a relatively coherent representation of who they are and what their values and long-term goals are. It is an inner story situated within a complex personality and self system which enables individuals to integrate their emotions, cognitions, and behaviours so that they can pursue and ultimately achieve their goals (McAdams, 1995, 2001; Singer & Blagov, 2004; Singer & Salovey, 1993). By integrating their reconstructed past, their present, and their imagined future, this identity gives individuals a sense of unity, continuity of the self, and direction or purpose in life (McAdams, 2013, 2015a, 2015b; McAdams & McLean, 2013; Singer, 2004).

Constructing a coherent self through autobiographical reasoning

The development of the life story is facilitated by the life story schema, a mental structure that represents individuals' organisation of their personal history and serves as "an interface between AM and the self" (Bluck & Habermas, 2000, p. 133). This schema is thought to be used during *autobiographical reasoning*, a form of meaning making which involves individuals interpreting their experiences and memories in a highly subjective way and linking them to each other and to changing or enduring aspects of themselves (Bluck & Habermas, 2000; Habermas & Bluck, 2000; McLean et al., 2007). Through autobiographical reasoning, individuals are able to draw inferences or semantic conclusions about the self from the episodic information contained in their memories (McAdams, 2013; McAdams & McLean, 2013). The aim is to construct a coherent narrative or plot around one's past experiences (especially around changes or life disruptions) that then informs the perception of the self as continuous or consistent across contexts and over time (Habermas & Köber, 2015; McAdams, 1996, 2013, 2015a; Syed & McLean, 2016).

There are four main types of coherence that individuals try to accomplish as they construct their life story: temporal, causal, thematic, and cultural (Habermas & Bluck, 2000; McAdams, 2015a). *Temporal coherence* involves ensuring that the experiences incorporated in the life story are organised in a specific (often chronological) sequence. *Causal coherence* involves ensuring that experiences are linked to each other and to self-characteristics in terms of cause and effect relationships. *Thematic coherence* involves linking experiences or life elements which seem to share common themes in terms of content or the goals that individuals were trying to reach in the experiences involved, such as agency (e.g., power, autonomy, achievement) and communion (e.g., love, intimacy, caring). Finally, *cultural coherence* is achieved by ensuring that one's life story follows the template of the normative life course in one's culture (e.g., when it comes to life phases or when specific major life events are expected to occur). Overall, coherence in the life story is important for the self and, as we will see in Chapter 4, for psychological well-being.

As mentioned earlier, the main way in which individuals achieve coherence is by engaging in autobiographical reasoning (Pasupathi, Mansour, & Brubaker, 2007). Linking memories to each other (e.g., based on themes) and to aspects of the self enables them to organise their life story and incorporate additional information into their sense of self. Over the years, researchers have developed different (often overlapping) ways of coding and analysing narratives of memories or life chapters in order to identify the links that individuals have established between their experiences and their sense of self. Below are some examples of these assessment methods.

Singer and Blagov (2000) distinguish between integrative and non-integrative memories. They conceptualise integrative memories as memories that individuals narrate by including statements about the meaning they have attached to the experience, for example about lessons learnt regarding the self, others, or life in general (*"The accident taught me that life is short and anything can happen at any time"*) or about deliberately using the memory to achieve a specific function (*"I always think about this memory if I'm going through a hard time because it reminds me of my strength"*). Such statements about meaning, lessons, or functional uses of the memory are absent from the narratives of non-integrative memories in Singer and Blagov's classification system.

Pasupathi and colleagues (2007) refer to the statements indicating links that individuals have made between their experiences and sense of self as *self-event connections*. They distinguish between self-event connections expressing stability in the self (e.g., showing how an event illustrates the self: *"That day spent looking after my ill friend shows that I am caring"*) and connections expressing a change in self-perception or in the self (*"I began to feel like a complete failure when I started putting on weight"*). McLean and Thorne (2003), on the other hand, focus on whether such connections indicate learning lessons or gaining insights from experiences. Lesson learning involves learning something new which may be used to guide behaviour in the future (*"My depressive episode and subsequent treatment taught me that I have to start taking care of myself"*). Gaining insights, on the other hand, involves becoming aware of something that may transform one's understanding of oneself or life in general (*"After getting the grades necessary to get into university, I realised that I'm not lazy at all; I actually can be very dedicated and work hard if I set my mind to something"*).

Continuing in a similar vein, Lilgendahl and McAdams (2011) focus on causal connections which emphasise how an experience has changed the self positively (e.g., by leading to growth) or negatively (e.g., by leading to a negative self-evaluation). This is partly related to redemption and contamination sequences in memory narratives (McAdams, Reynolds, Lewis, Patten, & Bowman, 2001). Redemption sequences indicate negative events given positive meaning because of a positive outcome or attribution (*"Being in an abusive relationship made me stronger and more independent; I will never put myself in the same situation again"*). In these sequences, what is negative about an experience is "redeemed, salvaged, mitigated, or made better in light of the ensuing good" (McAdams et al., 2001, p. 474). Contamination sequences, on the other hand, indicate positive events followed by negative outcomes (*"I loved being part of the cool kids' group in high school, but now I can see that it made me more conforming and more willing to change aspects of myself in order to fit in"*). In these sequences, what is good "is spoiled, ruined, contaminated, or undermined by what follows it" (McAdams et al., 2001, p. 474).

Finally, McLean and Fournier (2008) have mapped self-event connections to the layers of personality proposed by McAdams (e.g., 2015a). They distinguish between dispositional, value, outlook, and personal growth self-event connections. Dispositional self-event connections involve understanding the self in terms of dispositional traits (first layer of personality) while reasoning about an experience (*"Spending time with my friend, who is very trusting and trustworthy, made me realise how negative and cynical I am"*). Value connections involve understanding the self in terms of one's beliefs or morality (second layer of personality) (*"Tearing the lead from the stranger who was kicking his dog and letting the dog run free made me realise that I am willing to stand up for what is right"*). Outlook connections focus on understanding the self in terms of perspectives and attitudes (second layer of personality) (*"Thinking about that relationship – even though it is over – reminds me that true happiness is out there and although we may not be happy 100% of the time, life is worth fighting for"*). Personal growth connections are related to the third layer of personality and involve drawing conclusions about one's development (e.g., in terms of maturity, confidence) as a result of an experience (*"The break-up shattered my self-confidence"*).

As these examples show, individuals can draw different conclusions from their AMs. They can learn lessons which can shape their future behaviour. Alternatively, they can make self-event connections that help them understand who they are or how they have changed over time. These connections can be between their AMs and different aspects of their sense of self, including personality traits, values, attitudes, and growth. They can indicate positive or negative aspects of or changes in the self. As we will see in Chapter 4, the nature of these self-event connections has important implications for psychological well-being.

The role of age and culture in the development of autobiographical reasoning

The construction of the life story and the type of connections that individuals make between their memories and their sense of self can be affected by different factors, such as the type of memory and individuals' cognitive processing during the experience depicted in the memory. These factors will be discussed further in Chapter 4. For now, however, it is important to recognise the role of individuals' age and cultural or social context. This can help us appreciate better the gradual development of the life story across the lifespan.

Age. In a study investigating self-event connections and thematic coherence, McLean and Fournier (2008) found that making personal growth and outlook connections may require significant cognitive effort. They also found that the thematic coherence of participants' memory narratives was positively related to the level of cognitive effort (indicated by the use of phrases such as "reflected about") and to the likelihood of participants reporting personal growth connections. Although this study relied on participants' words to assess cognitive effort rather than objective cognitive measures, it does suggest that autobiographical reasoning is an effortful activity that may require com plex cognitive operations. This is in line with the evidence that autobiographical reasoning and the life story emerge in adolescence and young adulthood, when significant life experiences occur (many of them for the first time) and individuals develop the cognitive skills required to derive organising themes for their lives, to identify their transformation following specific experiences, and to understand what constitutes a typical life story in their culture (see Habermas & Bluck, 2000; Habermas & Reese, 2015; McAdams, 2013, 2015a, 2015b). In fact, coherence and the stability of AMs increase slowly following early adolescence (Bauer, Hättenschwiler, & Larkina, 2016; Habermas & Bluck, 2000; Habermas, Diel, & Welzer, 2013; Habermas & Reese, 2015; Larkina, Merrill, & Bauer, 2017). Self-continuity also increases over time as individuals develop more coherent life narratives, experience increasing stability in their personal characteristics and life circumstances, and are better able to perceive their past and their imagined future selves as similar to the present self (see Löckenhoff & Rutt, 2017).

Culture. Culture influences individuals as actors, motivated agents, and autobiographical authors (McAdams, 2013). It may set norms that regulate how the actor expresses his/her dispositional traits and provide information that guides the agent's articulation and pursuit of goals and values. In addition, it may provide the template and the tools that the author uses to construct the life story. As McAdams (2015a, p. 8) puts it, "We are the authors of our own unique stories, for sure, but we get plenty of editorial assistance, as well as resistance, from the social, ideological, and cultural world around us." Individuals' stories are in fact grounded in their social and cultural context (Hammack, 2008; McAdams, 1996, 2015a, 2015b; McAdams & Pals, 2006; McLean et al., 2017; McLean & Syed, 2015; Pasupathi et al., 2007). McLean and Syed (2015) propose that cultures contain *master narratives*, which are shared, relatively rigid stories providing information about these cultures (e.g., their history, goals, values, identity) and about how one is expected to live in them or to understand oneself. According to these authors, individuals internalise these narratives and negotiate them as they construct personal narratives which may be in line with the master narratives or represent alternatives to them (see also McLean et al., 2017).

The influence of master narratives can be seen in the role that *structural master narratives* and *cultural life scripts* play in the organisation of the life story. Structural master narratives focus on how stories should be constructed and told in one's culture, for example in terms of the detail they should contain or the plot they should follow as they seek resolution (McLean & Syed, 2015). In Western countries (especially in the United States) the redemption narrative – the story of the hero or heroine who overcomes adversity to achieve growth, maturity, or success in life – provides a powerful plot that guides how individuals interpret and recount adversity stories (see McAdams, 2015a, 2015b; McLean & Syed, 2015). Cultural life scripts, on the other hand, are shared representations of the order and time in which transitional events (e.g., going to school, getting married) are supposed to happen in a typical (idealised) life course (Berntsen & Rubin, 2004). They represent a type of master narrative that focuses on one's biography or on how life should unfold (McLean & Syed, 2015). These scripts may act as templates that guide the organisation and recall of AMs, especially those of transitional positive events (Berntsen & Rubin, 2004; Bohn & Habermas, 2016; Hatiboğlu & Habermas, 2016; Zaragoza Scherman, Salgado, Shao, & Berntsen, 2017). They may also affect the kind of future-oriented images of the self that individuals include in their life story (Rathbone, Salgado, Akan, Havelka, & Berntsen, 2016).

Master narratives are transmitted in several ways, including through family narratives and the media (Fivush & Merrill, 2016; Janssen & Haque, 2018; McLean et al., 2007; McLean & Syed, 2015; Merrill & Fivush, 2016). Family narratives consist of stories that members share with each other about events that they have experienced separately or together, for example a family holiday, parents' stories about their past, or children's stories about school. The stories that parents, grandparents, or older relatives share with younger family members (i.e., intergenerational narratives) are particularly important. Through such stories, older adults help young people understand themselves (especially where they come from and what their place in the world is), their family members, family dynamics and relationships, different ways of seeing the world, and what is considered acceptable or unacceptable in their culture (Fivush & Merrill, 2016; Merrill & Fivush, 2016). These stories also help develop shared family values and belief systems that are influenced by the broader cultural context (Fivush & Merrill, 2016) and are thus important for the development of the second layer of personality in the life story model. Finally, they help young people develop a specific way of understanding experiences and telling stories (Fivush & Merrill, 2016; McAdams, 2015a; McLean et al., 2007; Merrill &

Fivush, 2016). They teach individuals about the structural master narratives in their culture and shape the third layer of personality – the life story.

The life story as an evolving structure

As mentioned earlier, the life story – just like the self-as-social-actor and the self-as-motivated-agent – is constantly evolving (e.g., McAdams, 2001; McAdams & McLean, 2013). It changes over time as individuals' circumstances, understanding of themselves, and needs change and as new life experiences need to be processed and linked to the self (Bluck & Habermas, 2000; McAdams, 2015a; Pasupathi et al., 2007). Individuals constantly edit or add new chapters to it: they incorporate new memories into the life story, reinterpret remote memories, forget some experiences, or find that some themes holding experiences together are no longer relevant to them (Pasupathi et al., 2007; Singer, Blagov, Berry, & Oost, 2013). In addition, they may incorporate new or forget old *imagined* future events which may be associated with different lessons or future-oriented self-images (i.e., representations of the self) (see Jeunehomme & D'Argembeau, 2017; Rathbone, Conway, & Moulin, 2011).

To illustrate how a change in the life story may occur, imagine a person who has always thought that they are naïve because they had a rather sheltered childhood. Over time, this person may come to see themselves as honest rather than naïve and attribute this characteristic to the fact that their parents are honest people. This person will thus revise their idea of themselves and make a new causal connection between this new idea and perhaps experiences involving their parents that exemplify honesty. Similarly, a person who has trust issues and a "drawer" full of memories of experiences in which they felt betrayed or taken advantage of may establish relationships with people whom they deem trustworthy. The "trust memory drawer", therefore, may no longer be as important as before and the person may revise their life story, incorporating more positive relationship memories, positive beliefs about others originating from these memories, and perhaps a revised idea of themselves in relation to others. Any future-oriented images of the self as being perennially lonely and vulnerable to others' evil intentions may thus be discarded, together with any potential images of future events such as sitting alone in an empty house in old age.

The fact that the life story or narrative identity is a constant work in progress has important implications. It may be a negative thing on some occasions, for example when previously well-adjusted individuals draw negative conclusions about themselves, other people, or life in general from adverse memories and experience issues such as reduced self-esteem or anxiety. It may, however, be positive when previously struggling individuals make positive self-event connections and thus experience positive outcomes such as increased self-esteem. The implications of this malleability of the life story for psychological well-being and therapy will be discussed in greater detail in Chapters 4 and 5. Before we get to those chapters, it is important to understand how individuals decide (consciously or unconsciously) which AMs to use as building blocks in their life story. Are all AMs integrated into narrative identity? Do individuals have the cognitive resources (or time and motivation…) to retain for a long time, reflect on, and form self-event connections for all their experiences? The answer, of course, is *no*. The remainder of this chapter focuses on those "special" memories that make it into the life story.

Memory, goals, and the self-memory system

Understanding which memories become part of one's life story requires first and foremost the understanding that cognition and behaviour are driven by goals which direct individuals' attention and resources towards the tasks at hand and help them generate plans which will facilitate their attainment (Carver & Scheier, 1990; Conway, 2005; Conway, Meares, & Standart, 2004; Conway, Singer, et al., 2004; McAdams, 2015a, 2015b; Singer & Salovey, 1993). Over the years, motivation and goals have been conceptualised in different ways (see Austin & Vancouver, 1996; Emmons, 1997; Higgins, 2012; McAdams, 2015a). Broadly speaking, goals are internal representations of states (e.g., events, outcomes) that individuals strive to attain or avoid (Austin & Vancouver, 1996; Emmons, 1997). They may be conscious or unconscious (see Austin & Vancouver, 1996; Emmons, 1997). Martin A. Conway and colleagues (Conway, Meares, et al., 2004; Conway, Singer, et al., 2004) have suggested that goals are largely non-conscious processes, but we can be aware of their outputs (e.g., our actions) or the mental representations derived from them (e.g., mental images associated with specific goals).

As mentioned earlier in this chapter, in the life story model goals are conceived as personality components that start developing in middle childhood. They turn individuals into motivated agents who want to achieve (or avoid) something and who have a plan for doing so (McAdams, 2015a). In order to ensure that they are achieving their goals, motivated agents need to monitor their progress towards goal achievement and, if necessary, adjust their plans to enhance their chances of success (see Harkin et al., 2016). According to Conway (e.g.,

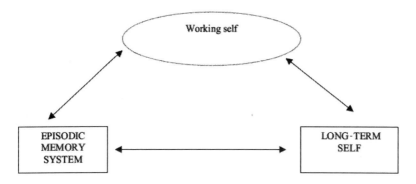

Figure 2.1 The structure of the self-memory system.
Source: "The Self and Autobiographical Memory: Correspondence and Coherence" by M. A. Conway, J. A. Singer, and A. Tagini, 2004, *Social Cognition, 22*(5), p. 494. Copyright 2004 by Guilford Press. Reprinted with permission of Guilford Press.

Conway, 2005, 2009; Conway & Pleydell-Pearce, 2000; Conway, Singer, et al., 2004), this monitoring can be unconscious and is made possible by the self-memory system (SMS), which consists of the episodic memory system, the long-term self, and the working self (see Figure 2.1).

The episodic memory system records (more or less truthfully) sensory, perceptual, conceptual, and affective elements of individuals' experience. In particular, it records and stores information that is relevant to individuals' short-term goals, for example goal generation, action planning, action outcomes, and outcome evaluations (see Conway, 2009; Williams, Conway, & Baddeley, 2008). The long-term self, which we mentioned earlier, consists of the autobiographical knowledge base and the conceptual self. The autobiographical knowledge base includes individuals' autobiographical knowledge, which is organised as general event knowledge structures (categories of events that share themes or are repeated, for example *my visits to my grandparents' village in Albania*), lifetime periods (extended periods reflecting overarching goals and activities, for example *my years as a student in Malta*), and the more global life story schema (Conway & Pleydell-Pearce, 2000; Conway, Singer, et al., 2004). This autobiographical knowledge is conceptual, concerned with long-term goals, and represented in memory independently of the experiences or contexts in which it was acquired (Williams et al., 2008), although the episodic memories that have become embedded in it are available for retrieval as

AMs (see Singer et al., 2013). The conceptual self consists of abstract knowledge that defines the self (Conway, Singer, et al., 2004). In the context of the life story model, it may be argued that the conceptual self contains primarily information about the self (e.g., insights, meanings) that individuals have extracted from their experiences through autobiographical reasoning.

The content of the long-term self is thought to be organised in the form of schemas, which are cognitive structures representing specific self-representations that have been experienced in the past (Conway, 2005; Markus, 1977). Based on earlier theories about individuals possessing multiple schemas or self-representations (e.g., Markus & Nurius, 1986; Markus & Ruvolo, 1989), the SMS model proposes that at any time a subset of these schemas – the working self – is active and modulates emotion, cognition, and behaviour. Individuals can switch between different working selves relatively rapidly, depending on the relevance of these working selves and the individuals' circumstances (Brown, Bailey, Stoll, & McConnell, 2016). Each working self consists of self-images (mental models of the self in relation to past, current, and future goals) and a hierarchy of goals (Conway, 2005; Conway, Singer, et al., 2004). Self-images may include, among other things, possible selves (e.g., representations of what one may become or fears becoming) (Markus & Nurius, 1986) or representations of what one believes they are (actual self), would like to be (ideal self), or thinks they should be (ought self) (Higgins, 1987). Working self goals, on the other hand, are thought to contain a standard or ideal, mechanisms for assessing the discrepancy between the standard and the current state, and plans for reducing or increasing this discrepancy (Conway, Singer, et al., 2004). They are involved in negative and positive feedback loops that help regulate behaviour (Carver & Scheier, 1990; Conway, Meares, et al., 2004). In negative feedback loops, the standard to which the current state of the individual is compared represents a desired state or outcome (e.g., doing well in an assignment). In this case, the plans generated by the working self aim to reduce the discrepancy between the actual state and the standard. In positive feedback loops, the standard represents a state or outcome that is to be avoided (e.g., making a fool of oneself in public), so the working self generates plans to increase the discrepancy between the actual state and the standard.

The working self goals are thought to modulate memory formation and storage (Conway & Pleydell-Pearce, 2000; Conway, Singer, et al., 2004). Through these goals, the working self organises individuals' psychological present: it evaluates the present circumstances (the actual state) and establishes priorities for goal processing and pursuit (Conway,

Singer, et al., 2004). It also monitors progress in goal attainment in the present and with regards to upcoming events (Conway & Loveday, 2015; Conway, Loveday, & Cole, 2016), thus helping determine the elements of the psychological present that are retained and become part of the autobiographical knowledge base. In fact, most episodic memories are lost shortly after their formation, typically within minutes or hours (Conway, 2009). Only memories that are relevant to individuals' long-term goals are retained in the long run (Conway, 2005; Conway, Singer, et al., 2004; Singer & Salovey, 1993), although some evidence (Thomsen et al., 2015) suggests that goal relevance may be less important for remembering and more important for whether events are perceived as central to the life story. Overall, goal-relevant memories tend to remain highly accessible in memory. They require a reduced amount of stimulation in order to be activated, that is move from a latent to an active state in which they can influence cognition and behaviour (see Eitam, Miele, & Higgins, 2013).

There are several potential explanations for the long-term storage and heightened accessibility of limited samples of experience that are related to goals. First, human cognitive resources are limited and retaining all the information we encounter on a daily basis is not sustainable. Second, goal-relevant memories tend to contain important information about the satisfaction of individuals' needs (e.g., the need to be autonomous, competent, and connected to others) and to be associated with intense affect. Progress towards goal achievement and information about need satisfaction contained in memories normally triggers positive affect, whereas goal obstruction or need thwarting are experienced as negative affect (Carver & Scheier, 1990; Conway, Singer, et al., 2004; Houle & Philippe, 2017; Singer & Salovey, 1993). Discrepancies between different domains of the self and, therefore, the failure to achieve desired self states (i.e., the ideal or ought self) may also be accompanied by negative emotional responses (Higgins, 1987; Higgins, Bond, Klein, & Strauman, 1986; Strauman & Higgins, 1987). This affective intensity may make goal-related memories more salient and thus more durable. Third, if we do attain a goal, we need to remember that we did so (so we do not continue to pursue it in vain) and how we did it (so we can use a similar strategy in the future) (Conway, Meares, et al., 2004). If we fail, on the other hand, we need to remember the experience so that we avoid the unsuccessful strategy we used and can learn lessons from it (Pillemer, 2003). In short, if we are to operate effectively in our environments and to strategically use AMs for the self and directive functions discussed in Chapter 1, we need to remember goal-relevant experiences.

Journey from episodic memory to the long-term self

The process whereby sensory-perceptual-conceptual-affective experiential details recorded by the episodic memory system become long-term memory representations can be explained by combining the SMS and the life story models. According to the SMS model, once the working self has determined that an episodic memory is goal-relevant, this memory may become integrated with the abstract autobiographical knowledge present in the long-term self (Conway & Pleydell-Pearce, 2000; Conway, Singer, et al., 2004). The autobiographical knowledge base may provide the conceptual context for this memory, for example by linking it to similar memories that share the same theme and by situating it into the relevant life period. Depending on its characteristics, such as its goal relevance and emotional intensity (see Thomsen et al., 2015), the memory may also contribute to the development of the life story once the individual subjects it to autobiographical reasoning and attempts to make lasting self-event connections. The memory and potentially the life period it is embedded in (Steiner, Thomsen, & Pillemer, 2017; Thomsen, 2015) may thus end up shaping individuals' narrative identity, personality, and sense of self.

As they become part of the long-term self, many of the newly-formed memories retain their links to the working self and its goals. Following autobiographical reasoning, they may also give rise to new self-images and goals which become part of the working self and shape the encoding and storing of future memories (Bluck & Habermas, 2000; Conway, 2005). There is significant evidence supporting this argument. In two studies involving older adults, Conway and Holmes (2004) found that individuals remember experiences that were relevant to their goals at the time these experiences occurred. The memories their participants reported for different life stages were closely related to the developmental challenges that they should have been facing in those stages according to Erikson's (1963) theory of psychosocial development. For example, memories from the second decade of life tended to revolve around identity issues, whereas memories from the third decade were mostly about achieving intimacy. Clare Rathbone and her colleagues have found that, when asked to generate AMs cued by current self-images (e.g., *"I am ambitious"*), individuals tend to report AMs of experiences that occurred around the time they think the self-images emerged (Rathbone, Moulin, & Conway, 2008) and that they tend to do the same when it comes to future self-images and future imagined events (Rathbone et al., 2011). Taken together, these findings suggest that memories retain their links to the working self and its goals and that, over time, past and future relevant AMs give rise to specific self-images.

Ultimately, some of the memories that the working self decides are important and need to be retained become *self-defining memories (SDMs)*. SDMs are highly vivid, affectively charged, and accessible memories which are closely linked to other memories (usually ones with which they share themes and affective sequences) and which focus on individuals' enduring concerns or unresolved conflicts (Singer & Salovey, 1993). Singer and Salovey (1993) argue that SDMs help individuals understand themselves and what matters to them because they are central to the life story and sense of self. They are associated with positive affect (e.g., happiness, pride) when they are about goal attainment and with negative affect (e.g., sadness, shame) when they are about goal non-attainment. As a result, they remind or inform individuals about the outcomes of specific goals they have pursued in the past and give rise to new long-term goals. They are particularly vivid and highly responsive to external (e.g., environmental) and internal (e.g., somatosensory) cues, so they can be easily accessed. Finally, as the definition states, they are linked to similar memories, partly because the SMS attempts to construct a coherent life story by interpreting these SDMs in ways that fit the existing narrative and ensuring that the individual maintains – as much as possible – a stable, coherent view of the self. In fact, maintaining a coherent sense of self is one of the key functions of the SMS (Conway, 2005; Conway, Singer, et al., 2004) and SDMs may help it fulfil this function. This is supported by evidence that individuals tend to report similar emotions and motives across their SDMs, regardless of their context and time at which they occurred (Sutin & Robins, 2005). They interpret their experiences "through a distinctive affective and motivational lens" (Sutin & Robins, 2005, p. 818), just as the SMS model proposes.

Blagov and Singer (2004) identify four dimensions of SDMs which have important implications for individuals' sense of self and psychological well-being: affect, specificity, content, and meaning. Affect refers to the valence and intensity of the emotions elicited when the SDM is retrieved (Blagov & Singer, 2004). Specificity refers to the amount of sensory and spatiotemporal detail contained in the memory (Blagov & Singer, 2004; Singer & Blagov, 2000). Specific SDMs describe in detail a unique event that happened within a 24-hour period, whereas non-specific SDMs describe in broad terms one or more events that happened over a long period of time or were repeated. The content of a SDM is related to its main theme and may refer to life-threatening events; exploration/recreation events; relationship events; achievement events; guilt/shame events or doing right vs doing wrong; drug, alcohol, or tobacco use; or unclassifiable events that do not fit into any of the other categories (Thorne & McLean, 2001). Finally, meaning refers to the extent to which individuals have drawn abstract meaning and learnt lessons from the experience depicted in the memory (Blagov & Singer, 2004; Singer & Blagov, 2000). As mentioned earlier in this chapter, integrative SDM narratives, unlike non-integrative ones, contain references to the meaning individuals have attached to the experience or lessons learnt from it. The relevance of affect, content, integrative meaning, and specificity for the self and well-being will be discussed in greater detail in Chapters 3 and 4.

Conclusion

In this chapter, we presented theories and empirical evidence showing that AM is inextricably linked to the self. Relying on the life story model of personality development, we discussed how individuals engage in autobiographical reasoning to extract meaning from their experiences and thus construct a narrative about who they have been, are, and may become. Using the SMS model, we then argued that not all experiences are subjected to autobiographical reasoning: although the episodic memory system records most or all of our experiences, only those experiences that are relevant for our long-term goals become part of our autobiographical knowledge and shape the life story and the self. Throughout the chapter, we focused primarily on the long-term impact of AM on the self and on the "mission" of the SMS to make sure that the life story and the self are coherent. In the next chapter, we focus on the *immediate* impact of AM retrieval on the self and discuss how AM performs its self and directive functions as it responds to internal and environmental stimuli on a daily basis.

References

Austin, J. T. & Vancouver, J. B. (1996). Goal constructs in psychology: Structure, process, and content. *Psychological Bulletin, 120*(3), 338–375.

Bauer, P. J., Hättenschwiler, N., & Larkina, M. (2016). "Owning" the personal past: Adolescents' and adults' autobiographical narratives and ratings of memories of recent and distant events. *Memory, 24*(2), 165–183.

Berntsen, D. & Rubin, D. C. (2004). Cultural life scripts structure recall from autobiographical memory. *Memory & Cognition, 32*, 427–442.

Blagov, P. S. & Singer, J. A. (2004). Four dimensions of SDMs (specificity, meaning, content, and affect) and their relationship to self-restraint, distress, and repressive defensiveness. *Journal of Personality, 72*(3), 481–511.

Bluck, S. & Habermas, T. (2000). The life story schema. *Motivation and Emotion, 24*(2), 121–147.

Bohn, A. & Habermas, T. (2016). Living in history and living by the cultural life script: How older Germans date their autobiographical memories. *Memory, 24*(4), 482–495.

Brown, C. M., Bailey, V. S., Stoll, H., & McConnell, A. R. (2016). Between two selves: Comparing global and local predictors of speed of switching between self-aspects. *Self and Identity, 15*(1), 72–89.

Carver, C. S. & Scheier, M. F. (1990). Origins and functions of positive and negative affect: A control-process view. *Psychological Review, 97*(1), 19–35.

Conway, M. A. (2005). Memory and the self. *Journal of Memory and Language, 53*(4), 594–628.

Conway, M. A. (2009). Episodic memories. *Neuropsychologia, 47*(11), 2305–2313.

Conway, M. A. & Holmes, A. (2004). Psychosocial stages and the accessibility of autobiographical memories across the life cycle. *Journal of Personality, 72*(3), 461–480.

Conway, M. A. & Loveday, C. (2015). Remembering, imagining, false memories & personal meanings. *Consciousness and Cognition, 33*, 574–581.

Conway, M. A., Loveday, C., & Cole, S. N. (2016). The remembering-imagining system. *Memory Studies, 9*(3), 256–265.

Conway, M. A., Meares, K., & Standart, S. (2004). Images and goals. *Memory, 12*(4), 525–531.

Conway, M. A. & Pleydell-Pearce, C. W. (2000). The construction of auto-biographical memories in the self-memory system. *Psychological Review, 107*(2), 261–288.

Conway, M. A., Singer, J. A., & Tagini, A. (2004). The self and autobiographical memory: Correspondence and coherence. *Social Cognition, 22*(5), 491–529.

Eitam, B., Miele, D. B., & Higgins, E. T. (2013). Motivated remembering: Remembering as accessibility and accessibility as motivational relevance. In D. E. Carlston (Ed.), *The Oxford handbook of social cognition* (pp. 463–475). New York, NY: Oxford University Press.

Emmons, R. A. (1997). Motives and life goals. In R. Hogan, J. Johnson, & S. Briggs (Eds.), *Handbook of personality psychology* (pp. 485–512). San Diego, CA: Academic Press.

Erikson, E. H. (1963). *Childhood and society (2nd ed.)*. New York, NY: Norton.

Fivush, R. & Merrill, N. (2016). An ecological systems approach to family narratives. *Memory Studies, 9*(3), 305–314.

Habermas, T. & Bluck, S. (2000). Getting a life: The emergence of the life story in adolescence. *Psychological Bulletin, 126*(5), 748–769.

Habermas, T., Diel, V., & Welzer, H. (2013). Lifespan trends of autobiograph-ical remembering: Episodicity and search for meaning. *Consciousness & Cognition, 22*, 1061–1072.

Habermas, T. & Köber, C. (2015). Autobiographical reasoning in life narratives buffers the effect of biographical disruptions on the sense of self-continuity. *Memory, 23*(5), 664–674.

Habermas, T. & Reese, E. (2015). Getting a life takes time: The development of the life story in adolescence and its precursors. *Human Development, 58,* 172–201.

Hammack, P. L. (2008). Narrative and the cultural psychology of identity. *Personality and Social Psychology Review, 12*(3), 222–247.

Harkin, B., Webb, T. L., Chang, B. P. I., Prestwich, A., Conner, M., et al. (2016). Does monitoring goal progress promote goal attainment? A meta-analysis of the experimental evidence. *Psychological Bulletin, 142*(2), 198–229.

Hatiboğlu, N. & Habermas, T. (2016). The normativity of life scripts and its relation with life story events across cultures and subcultures. *Memory, 24*(10), 1369–1381.

Higgins, E. T. (1987). Self-discrepancy: A theory relating self and affect. *Psychological Review, 94*(3), 319–340.

Higgins, E. T. (2012). *Beyond pleasure and pain: How motivation works.* New York, NY: Oxford University Press.

Higgins, E. T., Bond, R. N., Klein, R., & Strauman, T. (1986). Self-discrepancies and emotional vulnerability: How magnitude, accessibility, and type of discrepancy influence affect. *Journal of Personality and Social Psychology, 51*(1), 5–15.

Houle, I. & Philippe, F. L. (2017). Need satisfaction in episodic memories impacts mood at retrieval and well-being over time. *Personality and Individual Differences, 105,* 194–199.

James, W. (1862). *Psychology.* New York, NY: Henry Holt & Co.

Janssen, S. M. J. & Haque, S. (2018). The transmission and stability of cultural life scripts: A cross-cultural study. *Memory, 26*(1), 131–143.

Jeunehomme, O. & D'Argembeau, A. (2017). Accessibility and characteristics of memories of the future. *Memory, 25*(5), 666–676.

Larkina, M., Merrill, N. A., & Bauer, P. J. (2017). Developmental changes in consistency of autobiographical memories: Adolescents' and young adults' repeated recall of recent and distance events. *Memory, 25*(8), 1036–1051.

Leary, M. R. & Tangney, J. P. (2012). The self as an organizing construct in the behavioral and social sciences. In M. R. Leary & J. P. Tangney (Eds.), *Handbook of self and identity (2nd ed.)* (pp. 1–18). New York, NY: Guilford Press.

Lilgendahl, J. P. & McAdams, D. P. (2011). Constructing stories of self-growth: How individual differences in patterns of autobiographical reasoning relate to well-being in midlife. *Journal of Personality, 79*(2), 391–428.

Löckenhoff, C. E. & Rutt, J. L. (2017). Age differences in self-continuity: Converging evidence and directions for future research. *The Gerontologist, 57*(3), 396–408.

Luke, M. & Stopa, L. (2009). Psychological theories of the self and their application to clinical disorders. In L. Stopa (Ed.), *Imagery and the threatened self: Perspectives on mental imagery and the self in cognitive therapy* (pp. 15–64). London, England: Routledge.

Markus, H. (1977). Self-schemata and processing information about the self. *Journal of Personality and Social Psychology, 35*(2), 63–78.

Markus, H. R. & Kitayama, S. (2010). Cultures and selves: A cycle of mutual constitution. *Perspectives on Psychological Science, 5*(4), 420–430.

Markus, H. & Nurius, P. (1986). Possible selves. *American Psychologist, 41*, 954–969.

Markus, H. & Ruvolo, A. (1989). Possible selves: Personalized representations of goals. In I., A. Pervin (Ed.), *Goal concepts in personality and social psychology* (pp. 211–242). Hillsdale, NJ: Erlbaum.

McAdams, D. P. (1985). *Power, intimacy, and the life story: Personological inquiries into identity.* New York, NY: Guilford Press.

McAdams, D. P. (1995). What do we know when we know a person? *Journal of Personality, 63*(3), 365–396.

McAdams, D. P. (1996). Personality, modernity, and the storied self: A contemporary framework for studying persons. *Psychological Inquiry, 7*(4), 295–321.

McAdams, D. P. (2001). The psychology of life stories. *Review of General Psychology, 5,* 100–122.

McAdams, D. P. (2008). Personal narratives and the life story. In O. P. John, R. W. Robins, & L. A. Pervin (Eds.), *Handbook of personality: Theory and research (3rd ed.)* (pp. 242–262). New York, NY: Guilford Press.

McAdams, D. P. (2013). The psychological self as actor, agent, and author. *Perspectives on Psychological Science, 8*(3), 272–295.

McAdams, D. P. (2015a). *The art and science of personality development.* New York, NY: Guilford Press.

McAdams, D. P. (2015b). Three lines of personality development: A conceptual itinerary. *European Psychologist, 20*(4), 252–264.

McAdams, D. P. & McLean, K. C. (2013). Narrative identity. *Current Directions in Psychological Science, 22*(3), 233–238.

McAdams, D. P. & Pals, J. L. (2006). A new Big Five: Fundamental principles for an integrative science of personality. *American Psychologist, 61*(3), 204–217.

McAdams, D. P., Reynolds, J., Lewis, M., Patten, A., & Bowman, P. J. (2001). When bad things turn good and good things turn bad: Sequences of redemption and contamination in life narrative, and their relation to psychosocial adaptation in midlife adults and in students. *Personality and Social Psychology Bulletin, 27,* 472–483.

McLean, K. C. & Fournier, M. A. (2008). The content and processes of autobiographical reasoning in narrative identity. *Journal of Research in Personality, 42,* 527–545.

McLean, K. C., Lilgendahl, J. P., Fordham, C., Alpert, E., Marsden, E., et al. (2017). Identity development in cultural context: The role of deviating from master narratives. *Journal of Personality.* Advance online publication.

McLean, K. C., Pasupathi, M., & Pals, J. L. (2007). Selves creating stories creating selves: A process model of self-development. *Personality and Social Psychology Review, 11*(3), 262–278.

McLean, K. C. & Syed, M. (2015). Personal, master, and alternative narratives: An integrative framework for understanding identity development in context. *Human Development, 58*(6), 318–349.

McLean, K. C. & Thorne, A. (2003). Late adolescents' self-defining memories about relationships. *Developmental Psychology, 39*(4), 635–645.

Merrill, N. & Fivush, R. (2016). Intergenerational narratives and identity across development. *Development Review, 40*, 72–92.

Morf, C. C. & Mischel, W. (2012). The self as a psycho-social dynamic processing system: Toward a converging science of selfhood. In M. R. Leary & J. P. Tangney (Eds.), *Handbook of self and identity (2nd ed.)* (pp. 21–49). New York, NY: Guilford Press.

Oyserman, D., Elmore, K., & Smith, G. (2012). Self, self-concept, and identity. In M. R. Leary & J. P. Tangney (Eds.), *Handbook of self and identity (2nd ed.)* (pp. 69–104). New York, NY: Guilford Press.

Pasupathi, M., Mansour, E., & Brubaker, J. R. (2007). Developing a life story: Constructing relations between self and experience in autobiographical narratives. *Human Development, 50*(2–3), 85–110.

Pillemer, D. (2003). Directive functions of autobiographical memory: The guiding power of the specific episode. *Memory, 11*(2), 193–202.

Rathbone, C. J., Conway, M. A., & Moulin, C. J. (2011). Remembering and imagining: The role of the self. *Consciousness and Cognition, 20*(4), 1175–1182.

Rathbone, C. J., Moulin, C. J., & Conway, M. A. (2008). Self-centered memories: The reminiscence bump and the self. *Memory & Cognition, 36*(8), 1403–1414.

Rathbone, C. J., Salgado, S., Akan, M., Havelka, J., & Berntsen, D. (2016). Imagining the future: A cross-cultural perspective on possible selves. *Consciousness and Cognition, 42*, 113–124.

Singer, J. A. (2004). Narrative identity and meaning making across the adult lifespan: An introduction. *Journal of Personality, 72*(3), 437–459.

Singer, J. A. & Blagov, P. S. (2000). *Classification system and scoring manual for self-defining autobiographical memories.* Unpublished manuscript, Department of Psychology, Connecticut College, New London, CT.

Singer, J. A. & Blagov, P. (2004). The integrative function of narrative processing: Autobiographical memories, self-defining memories and the life story theory of identity. In D. Beike, J. Lampinen, & D. Behrend (Eds.), *The self and memory* (pp. 117–138). New York, NY: The Psychology Press.

Singer, J. A., Blagov, P., Berry, M., & Oost, K. M. (2013). Self-defining memories, scripts, and the life story: Narrative identity in personality and psychotherapy. *Journal of Personality, 81*(6), 569–582.

Singer, J. A. & Salovey, P. (1993). *The remembered self: Emotion and memory in personality.* New York, NY: Free Press.

Steiner, K. L., Thomsen, D. K., & Pillemer, D. B. (2017). Life story chapters, specific memories, and conceptions of the self. *Applied Cognitive Psychology, 31*(5), 478–487.

Strauman, T. J. & Higgins, E. T. (1987). Automatic activation of self-discrepancies and emotional syndromes: When cognitive structures influence affect. *Journal of Personality and Social Psychology, 53*(6), 1004–1014.

Sutin, A. R. & Robins, R. W. (2005). Continuity and correlates of emotions and motives in self-defining memories. *Journal of Personality, 73*(3), 793–824.

Swann, W. B. & Bosson, J. K. (2010). Self and identity. In S. T. Fiske, D. T. Gilbert, & G. Lindzey (Eds.), *Handbook of social psychology* (5th ed., pp. 589–628). New York, NY: McGraw-Hill.

Syed, M. (2017). Advancing the cultural study of personality and identity: Models, methods, and outcomes. *Current Issues in Personality Psychology, 5*(1), 65–72.

Syed, M. & McLean, K. C. (2016). Understanding identity integration: Theoretical, methodological, and applied issues. *Journal of Adolescence, 47,* 109–118.

Thomsen, D. K. (2015). Autobiographical periods: A review and central components of a theory. *Review of General Psychology, 19*(3), 294–310.

Thomsen, D. K., Jensen, T., Holm, T., Olesen, M. H., Schnieber, A., & Tønnesvang, J. (2015). A 3.5 year diary study: Remembering and life story importance are predicted by different event characteristics. *Consciousness and Cognition, 36,* 180–195.

Thorne, A. & McLean, K. C. (2001). *Manual for coding events in SDMs.* Unpublished manuscript, University of California, Santa Cruz, CA.

Williams, H. L., Conway, M. A., & Baddeley, A. D. (2008). The boundaries of episodic memories. In T. F. Shipley & J. M. Zacks (Eds.), *Understanding events: From perception to action* (pp. 589–616). New York, NY: Oxford University Press.

Zaragoza Scherman, A., Salgado, S., Shao, Z., & Berntsen, D. (2017). Life script events and autobiographical memories of important life story events in Mexico, Greenland, China, and Denmark. *Journal of Applied Research in Memory and Cognition, 6*(1), 60–73.

3 Not just a long-term affair: How autobiographical memory retrieval exerts an immediate influence on the self

Introduction

In the previous chapters, we argued that one of the main functions of autobiographical memory (AM) is to contribute to the development of a coherent sense of self and that it achieves this function throughout the lifespan, as individuals process their experiences and derive meanings from them (Bluck, Alea, Habermas, & Rubin, 2005; Bluck & Habermas, 2000; Conway, 2005; McAdams, 2013, 2015). We also presented the self-memory system (SMS) (e.g., Conway, 2005; Conway, Singer, & Tagini, 2004), which is conceptualised as consisting of an episodic memory system that records day-to-day experiences, a long-term self containing conceptual autobiographical knowledge and information about the self, and a working self consisting of long-term self goals and self-images that are active at any one time. We stated that one of the aims of the SMS is to preserve a stable, coherent sense of self and that it achieves this aim in different ways, for example by encoding and interpreting experiences in ways that fit the current life story. If someone has interpreted several interactions with others as involving rejection and indicating that they are unlovable, they can maintain this view of themselves by interpreting other interpersonal interactions in the same way, regardless of whether they involve rejection or not.

As important as self-coherence and stability are, maintaining the status quo is not beneficial at all times. As the example above suggests, the self-images and beliefs that the SMS tries to preserve can some-times be negative. In these cases, as we will see in Chapter 4, change may be needed to alleviate the psychological distress that results from the persistent negative self-views. Change is also needed on a day-to-day or moment-to-moment basis as we adapt to our changing environments and to a "never-ceasing flow of external and internal stimuli" (Singer & Salovey, 1993, p. 6). On a daily basis, we encounter stimuli such as music (Belfi, Karlan, & Tranel, 2016), objects (Zijlema, van den Hoven, & Eggen, 2017), or physical scars (Cockerham, Çili, & Stopa, 2016) that trigger the retrieval of particular AMs. We have to solve problems, manage our emotions, or evaluate our surroundings and behave accordingly. In order to achieve our short- and long-term goals, we have to adequately respond to stimuli and adapt to different situations. These tasks are facilitated by AM as it fulfils its self and directive functions.

The response to internal or external stimuli is thought to be planned and executed by the SMS. In fact, according to the SMS model, the key functions of the SMS are to preserve a stable sense of self while also helping individuals adapt to their current circumstances (Conway, 2005). The latter function, *adaptive correspondence*, involves the SMS recording ongoing goal activity and responding to internal or environmental demands to ensure individuals' fitness and survival (Conway, 2005; Conway, Singer, et al., 2004). This function is achieved by the working self, the online representation of the self that modulates individuals' cognitive, affective, and behavioural responses. One way to understand how this happens, and how AM achieves its self and directive functions, is through the literature on the immediate impact of AM retrieval on individuals. In the first part of this chapter, we review the empirical evidence on the impact of AM retrieval on affect, aspects of the self, and behaviour. In the second part, we discuss this evidence in light of the SMS model.

Impact of memory retrieval on affect

Evidence suggests that the retrieval of different types of AMs (e.g., self-defining and non-self-defining memories, voluntary and involuntary ones) can elicit physiological (Berntsen & Hall, 2004; Wisco et al., 2015) and emotional responses (Berntsen & Hall, 2004; Boals, Hathaway, & Rubin, 2011; del Palacio-Gonzalez, Berntsen, & Watson, 2017; Gillihan, Kessler, & Farah, 2007; Greenhoot, Sun, Bunnell, & Lindboe, 2013; Houle & Philippe, 2017; Nelis, Holmes, Palmieri, Bellelli, & Raes, 2015; Öner & Gülgöz, 2018; Philippe, Koestner, Lecours, Beaulieu-Pelletier, & Bois, 2011; Philippot, Schaefer, & Herbette, 2003; Ritchie, Skowronski, Cadogan, & Sedikides, 2014; Schaefer & Philippot, 2005). Overall, research shows that the retrieval of positive AMs is associated with positive affect, whereas the retrieval of negative AMs can elicit negative affect. Partly because of this, positive AMs may be effective as a mood repair tool (Hetherington & Moulds, 2015; Josephson, Singer, & Salovey, 1996; Öner & Gülgöz, 2018).

The emotional response to AM retrieval is partly related to memories' relationship with individuals' goals and needs, in particular with the extent to which the memory represents goal attainment or non-attainment and the satisfaction or thwarting of basic psychological needs, such as the need for autonomy, feeling connected to others, and feeling competent (Houle & Philippe, 2017; Philippe et al., 2011; Singer & Salovey, 1993). Houle and Philippe (2017) argue that the level of need satisfaction experienced during an event may be encoded in memory and remain attached to it. According to these authors, the retrieval of a memory may reactivate the level of need satisfaction that was experienced when the event occurred, thus triggering the emotional response. This is in line with Singer and Salovey's (1993) argument that, by eliciting emotion, self-defining memories (SDMs) remind us what it feels like to achieve or fail to achieve an important goal. Positive SDMs are generally characterised by a greater level of need satisfaction than negative ones (Philippe, Bouizegarene, Guilbault, Rajotte, & Houle, 2015) and are generally about attained goals (Singer & Salovey, 1993), although negative memories can also represent the satisfaction of some needs and elicit positive affect (Houle & Philippe, 2017).

Other characteristics of the retrieved AMs can determine their affective impact. To begin with, the negative affect associated with AMs fades more rapidly than the positive affect (a phenomenon termed *fading affect bias* or *FAB*), potentially because individuals are driven to maintain a positive view of their experiences and of themselves (see Lindeman, Zengel, & Skowronski, 2017; Ritchie et al., 2015; Skowronski, Walker, Henderson, & Bond, 2014; Walker, Skowronski, & Thompson, 2003). An implication of this bias is that individuals may experience more intense affective responses after recalling positive AMs than negative ones, but there are exceptions to the general FAB pattern. Negative experiences perceived as being psychologically close (Öner & Gülgöz, 2018), unresolved, or important for the self (Skowronski et al., 2014) may retain their affective charge and still trigger intense negative affect. This, as we will see in Chapter 4, is highly relevant to the clinical domain.

Memory specificity, content, meaning, and voluntary vs involuntary nature can also affect reactions to memory retrieval. When it comes to specificity, the intensity of the emotions experienced at retrieval is positively related to the sensory detail present in negative memories, but not in positive ones (Schaefer & Philippot, 2005). The retrieval of specific SDMs is associated with a greater increase in negative affect than the retrieval of non-specific SDMs (Lardi, D'Argembeau, Chanal, Ghisletta, & Van der Linden, 2010). The affect elicited by SDMs can also vary depending on their content with, for example, life-threatening events triggering significant increases in negative affect (Lardi et al., 2010). Findings regarding the importance of meaning are inconsistent, but some tend to indicate a positive influence of this dimension. Post-recall situational well-being, for example, is positively associated with integrative meaning and negatively associated with contamination sequences when the recalled SDM is positive (Philippe et al., 2015). Open memories (emotional memories one has not come to terms with) may elicit more intense emotions than closed memories, which may be integrative (Beike, Adams, & Wirth-Beaumont, 2007; Beike & Wirth-Beaumont, 2005). Describing adverse memories by expressing one's subjective perspective on these memories (especially in terms of positive impact) may also be accompanied by lower levels of distress (Greenhoot et al., 2013). Finally, the retrieval of involuntary memories can have a greater emotional impact than the retrieval of voluntary memories (Berntsen & Hall, 2004; del Palacio-Gonzalez et al., 2017; Watson, Berntsen, Kuyken, & Watkins, 2012).

Impact of memory retrieval on the self

In addition to affective states, memory retrieval can also affect perceptions of the self in the here and now. Some evidence suggests that recalling AMs increases self-concept accessibility and may lead individuals to describe themselves with more psychological, trait-related information than the retrieval of knowledge that is not personally relevant (Charlesworth, Allen, Havelka, & Moulin, 2016). This means that AM retrieval may influence the type of self-concept that is subsequently experienced and reported. Indeed, focusing on memories related to specific traits can influence the type of self-concept individuals report in relation to these traits (Fazio, Effrein, & Falender, 1981). Self-concept content may also be influenced temporarily by the perceived desirability of certain attributes, which may trigger a search for, and retrieval of, memories that reflect these attributes (Kunda & Sanitioso, 1989).

Memory recall can also affect self-evaluations. Jennings and McLean (2013) found that participants were able to repair their state self-esteem following a self-threat (false feedback suggesting that they were prejudiced) after recalling positive memories and memories demonstrating that they were tolerant. Beike, Kleinknecht, and Wirth-Beaumont (2004) found that individuals with open memories report lower self-esteem than individuals with closed memories. They also tend to describe the self with fewer positive words and more internal-referent words (e.g., words referring to emotions and thoughts) after recalling open memories than after recalling closed ones. Strelan and Zdaniuk

(2015) found that recalling events in which individuals were made to feel like a failure by another person was associated with low state self-esteem, whereas recalling events in which they felt proud of themselves was associated with high state self-esteem. Ritchie, Sedikides, and Skowronski (2016) found that the retrieval of positive memories was associated with higher state self-esteem than the retrieval of negative memories. Similarly, we found that participants reported higher state self-esteem after recalling a positive SDM than after recalling a negative one (Çili & Stopa, 2015). They also reported a higher proportion of self-cognitions referring to emotional states after recalling a non-integrative SDM (i.e., an SDM they described without referring to meanings or lessons learnt) than after recalling an integrative one. More recently, Austin and Costabile (2017) found that participants recalling positive agentic events (i.e., events related to personal achievements) reported greater post-recall state self-esteem than participants recalling positive communal events (i.e., events related to relationships).

The retrieval of different memories can also affect other self-related variables. Ritchie and his colleagues (2016) found that the retrieval of positive memories was also associated with higher levels of perceived meaningfulness in life and self-continuity (i.e., coherence and stability in one's sense of self) than the retrieval of negative memories. Hallford and Mellor (2016) found that state self-esteem, current perceptions of meaning in life, state self-efficacy, and awareness of having a life story increased, and negative affect decreased, for participants who recalled an experience of successfully coping with a challenge. Participants who recalled an experience that had shaped their identity also reported increased positive affect, self-esteem, meaning, and self-efficacy afterwards.

To summarise, memory retrieval affects the way in which individuals describe and evaluate the self. Overall, evidence suggests that recalling positive memories or memories associated with achievements can have a positive impact on state self-esteem, as well as on self-efficacy and perceptions of meaningfulness and continuity of the self. Recalling negative memories, on the other hand, can have a negative transient impact on self-perceptions.

Impact of memory retrieval on behaviour

Given their relationship with goals, AMs may also affect the goals individuals report following retrieval. We found that the goals individuals report as important for them to achieve may be different after they recall positive compared with negative SDMs (Çili & Stopa, 2015, Study

2). Our participants reported a marginally higher proportion of goals related to recreational or exploration activities (e.g., *travel the world*) and a marginally lower proportion of achievement goals requiring effortful activity (e.g., *get a PhD*) after recalling a positive SDM than after recalling a negative one. These differences did not reach statistical significance, but our findings are somewhat consistent with those of Seto, Hicks, Vess, and Geraci (2016), who found that recalling vivid memories of mortality-related experiences influenced the importance of the goals and strivings that participants reported following the recall. According to these authors, remembering experiences related to mortality may activate highly important personal goals and thus encourage individuals to pursue these goals in order to live a meaningful, authentic life.

In addition to goals, memory retrieval can influence optimism and behavioural intentions. Austin and Costabile (2017) found that recalling positive personal achievements was associated with greater post-recall optimism than the recall of positive communal memories. Similarly, Cheung and colleagues (2013) found that recalling nostalgic memories can increase optimism for the future. Hallford and Mellor (2016) did not find changes in optimism following memory retrieval, but this may have been due to the fact that they assessed optimism using a single-item measure which may not have been sensitive enough to detect such changes. Based on the findings of Austin and Costabile and Cheung and colleagues, and on evidence regarding the impact of optimism on behaviour in the long run (see Carver, Scheier, & Segerstrom, 2010), it is reasonable to argue that feeling optimistic following the retrieval of an AM can influence behaviour. In addition to potentially influencing behaviour through optimism, AM retrieval can influence behavioural intentions. Strelan and Zdaniuk (2015), for example, found that recalling negative memories such as being a victim of a transgression (e.g., being made to feel like a failure by another person) may be associated with a reduced intention to forgive, whereas recalling positive experiences in which one felt proud of oneself may encourage individuals to forgive personally experienced transgressions.

In line with the literature on the directive function of AM, memories can also exert an immediate impact on individuals' behaviour. For example, thinking about memories in a way that makes them feel open and unresolved can make individuals engage in a greater number of memory-related behaviours (e.g., donating to charity), perhaps because open memories are usually related to goals that the individual is yet to achieve (Beike, Adams, & Naufel, 2010). Recalling an instance of a public speaking success can facilitate present public speaking performance, whereas recalling a success memory that is not relevant to public speaking may not (Pezdek & Salim, 2011). Recalling academic general success memories and specific failure memories enhances performance on cognitive tests compared to recalling general failure memories and specific success memories, arguably because general memories are more likely to help individuals infer global aptitudes and to be seen as typical of the self than specific memories (Selimbegović, Régner, Huguet, & Chatard, 2016; Selimbegović, Régner, Sanitioso, & Huguet, 2011).

Additional factors influencing the impact of retrieval

As the previous sections have shown, not all memories affect individuals in the same way upon retrieval. Memory characteristics (e.g., valence, affective intensity, specificity, content, meaning making, voluntary or involuntary nature) can have a significant impact on how individuals feel and behave afterwards. Other factors may also be involved, but the evidence is limited as this is still a relatively new research area. Nevertheless, it is important to review some of this evidence in order to understand the complexity of the transient effects of memory retrieval on the self. In this section, we focus on culture, individuals' psychological well-being at the time of retrieval, and the way in which individuals process the memories when they retrieve them.

Culture. Individuals' cultural background may influence how they respond to memory retrieval. Some support for this argument comes from a study in which Tsai and Lau (2013) asked Asian American and European American students to recall an experience of interpersonal rejection, failure to achieve an important goal, or walking through a building. Results showed that Asian American participants were more distressed following the recall of the rejection memories than their European American counterparts. In addition, insight into the rejection memories was positively associated with post-recall distress among Asian Americans, but not among European Americans. These findings need to be replicated with non-student populations and with individuals from different cultures before we can draw any significant conclusions regarding the importance of culture for AM retrieval. Nevertheless, they do suggest that individuals may respond to the retrieval of AMs depending on how the experiences depicted in these memories are valued and interpreted in their culture. Remembering experiences of being rejected by members of their social groups may be more distressing for individuals coming from interdependent cultures that value harmonious interpersonal relationships than for individuals coming from individualistic cultures.

Psychological well-being. Individuals' psychological well-being at the time of retrieval can affect how they respond to their memories. It is plausible to argue that healthy individuals and individuals suffering from a psychological disorder may react differently to thinking about a distressing or a positive memory. To date, however, the evidence we have concerns primarily the effects of thinking about positive AMs in individuals experiencing dysphoria or depression. While some studies (e.g., Hetherington & Moulds, 2015; Nelis et al., 2015) have found evidence of mood repair following positive AM retrieval regardless of dysphoria or depressive symptoms, others have not. Overall, the literature suggests that individuals experiencing dysphoria or depression (and, sometimes, formerly depressed individuals) can experience limited or no mood repair after recalling a positive AM (Joorman & Siemer, 2004; Joorman, Siemer, & Gotlib, 2007; Vanderlind, Stanton, Weinbrecht, Velkoff, & Joorman, 2017). Depressed individuals can actually experience increased sadness (Joorman et al., 2007). Dysphoric individuals can also experience a more intense response to voluntary and involuntary memory retrieval (at least in terms of anger, fear, and sadness) than non-depressed individuals (del Palacio-Gonzalez et al., 2017).

There are different explanations as to why dysphoric or depressed individuals are less likely to benefit from the mood repair power of positive AMs. A review of these explanations is beyond the scope of this book. Overall, however, researchers tend to focus on the fact that recalling positive memories may trigger ruminative processes in these individuals, leading them to compare their current situation to their happier past and thus experience negative affect (Joorman & Siemer, 2004). In addition, these individuals can experience a fear of positive emotion, preferring negative emotions that are more in line with their current mood and self-perceptions (Vanderlind et al., 2017). This explanation is partly supported by evidence that depressed individuals can experience a reduction in sadness after recalling a positive AM if this memory is self-concordant (i.e., it represents a past self that matches their current self) (Werner-Seidler, Tan, & Dalgleish, 2017). These findings suggest that positive AMs and the consequences of their retrieval may be incongruent with how individuals experiencing psychological distress perceive themselves. As a result, they may fail to elicit positive reactions upon retrieval.

Processing style. Evidence suggests that the impact of AM retrieval can vary, depending on whether individuals process the memories using an abstract analytical style (i.e., focusing on causes, meanings, and outcomes) or a concrete experiential style (i.e., focusing on sensory elements and bodily experience). Although some studies (Hetherington & Moulds, 2015; Nelis et al., 2015, Study 2; Werner-Seidler & Moulds, 2014) have found that positive AM retrieval can lead to mood repair regardless of the processing mode individuals adopt, other studies suggest that adopting the experiential mode while processing positive AMs can have a more positive impact on post-retrieval mood than analytical processing (Gadeikis, Bos, Schweizer, Murphy, & Dunn, 2017; Nelis et al., 2015, Study 1; Seebauer et al., 2016). The differences between these studies may be due to methodological issues and the type of memories that participants were asked to retrieve. For example, some authors (Nelis et al., 2015; Werner-Seidler & Moulds, 2014) argue that, although the experiential processing mode may be more beneficial overall, the analytical mode may also be beneficial when the positive memories are relevant and meaningful for individuals' sense of self.

Impact of AM retrieval explained through the SMS model

As the previous sections have shown, recalling different types of AMs can have a significant influence on individuals' emotional states, self-perceptions, and behaviour. At this point, it is legitimate to ask: How can memories of experiences that have happened months or years ago influence us in the present? Why do they make us feel and behave in a particular way, depending on their and our characteristics? (Also, going back to our Introduction, how can one refuse £1 million just to avoid thinking about past experiences?) In the remainder of this chapter, we will attempt to answer these questions.

A good point at which to start understanding the impact of memory retrieval is the concept of *autonoesis* or *autonoetic consciousness* that we introduced in Chapter 1. Autonoetic consciousness is a form of consciousness that enables individuals to become aware of and mentally represent their subjective experiences across time (Tulving, 1985, 2002; Wheeler, Stuss, & Tulving, 1997). It enables us to mentally travel in time, reliving past experiences or imagining future experiences from our perspective while being aware of the subjective time in which events happened or are likely to happen. It thus helps us to achieve an awareness of the self in the past, present, and future and to draw on our AMs as we plan for the future (see Wheeler et al., 1997). This feature of AM, together with the SMS model, can help us understand what happens when we remember past experiences.

As mentioned earlier, the SMS helps individuals achieve adaptive correspondence (i.e., adapt to their environments) while preserving self-coherence (Conway, 2005; Conway, Singer, et al., 2004). The working self is thought to help the SMS accomplish and maintain a balance between these two seemingly conflicting tasks by guiding individuals' responses to shifts in environmental demands that may be signalled by external or internal cues. The goals of the working self, as described in Chapter 2, are thought to be involved in positive and negative feedback loops which regulate behaviour by increasing or decreasing the discrepancy between the individual's actual state and a standard (Conway, Meares, & Standart, 2004), depending on whether the related self-images reflect standards that are to be avoided or approached. It is these goals and the related self-images making up the working self that can explain the impact of memory retrieval on individuals.

The working self organises and manages goal processes while it evaluates current experience (especially progress in goal attainment) and specifies action sequences that enable individuals to adapt to this experience (Conway, Singer, et al., 2004). Conway, Singer, et al. (2004) propose that, when faced with a new situation or stimulus (e.g., after completing a task or moving to a new environment), the individual's goals change. Any transition in goal status, whether it is achievement or blocking of goals, triggers an affective response and can potentially challenge self-coherence. When this happens, the SMS has to adapt and respond to the transition. The working self evaluates the goal status change and goes into retrieval mode as it searches through the long-term self's autobiographical knowledge base and the episodic memory system for past episodes related to the current transition (see Figure 3.1). The search finally yields a particular AM (typically a self-defining one), together with a related working self, a goal-action-outcome sequence, and an affective response. A new working self is thus activated and provides the goal-relevant cognitive and affective information that is needed to respond to the current circumstances. These circumstances may then be interpreted in the light of past experience. This means that the newly created episodic memory of these circumstances may fit the narrative sequence of the activated past memory. If it contains information that is relevant for the long-term goals, this episodic memory will be retained and embedded in memory networks that share its thematic narrative. The interaction of the long-term self and the episodic memory system, which is mediated by the working self, will thus yield a new memory from which abstract knowledge about the self, others, and the world can be derived. Once this is accomplished, the working self will have helped achieve both correspondence and self-coherence.

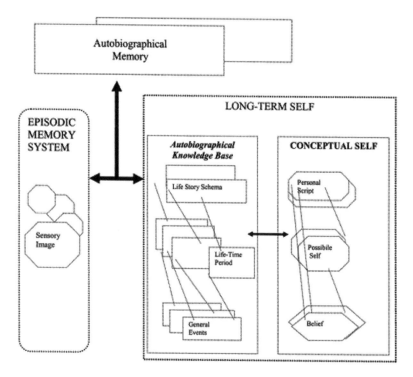

Figure 3.1 Generation of autobiographical memories.

Source: "The Self and Autobiographical Memory: Correspondence and Coherence," by M. A. Conway, J. A. Singer, and A. Tagini, 2004, *Social Cognition, 22*(5), p. 498. Copyright 2004 by Guilford Press. Reprinted with permission of Guilford Press.

This account is in line with theoretical and empirical work suggesting that memories can be accessed (and then go on to influence cognition and behaviour) if they are relevant to the current goals and can help individuals achieve them (see Eitam & Higgins, 2010; Eitam, Miele, & Higgins, 2013). It is also supported by evidence that individuals' current goals can influence whether positive or negative self-knowledge becomes more accessible and is activated (Scholer, Ozaki, & Higgins, 2014) and that memories which are congruent with the currently active self-image are more easily retrieved than incongruent or less relevant memories (Rathbone & Moulin, 2017). However, the SMS model does not stop at the moment of memory activation. It helps us understand what happens *after* activation. Based on this model and the existing literature, we have argued that the retrieval of particular memories – especially SDMs – may trigger the activation of related working selves while inhibiting the activation of non-relevant memories and working selves associated to them (Çili & Stopa, 2015). Specifically, we have argued that the working self-images and goals influence individuals' reactions to memory retrieval. In this account, the self-images of the newly-activated working self contain specific beliefs about the self or others (e.g., *"I am inadequate"*) and are evaluated positively or negatively by individuals, depending on whether the associated memory represents goal attainment or non-attainment. As McAdams (2013) argues, self-esteem is related to the self's success or failure as a motivated agent. As a result, the activation of a memory associated with achievement or failure is likely to produce a change in individuals' state self-esteem.

When it comes to goals, in line with the SMS model, we have suggested that the goals of the newly-activated working self drive the behavioural response to the memory retrieval (Çili & Stopa, 2015). Some evidence indicates that self-esteem might mediate the relationship between recalled memories and behavioural intentions (see Strelan & Zdaniuk, 2015). Nevertheless, the goals of the working self as conceptualised in the SMS model are supposed to directly guide behaviour. Beike and colleagues (2010) state that thinking about memories in a way that makes them feel unresolved (and therefore associated with unattained goals) may encourage individuals to engage in memory-related behaviours so that they can achieve the associated goals. When it comes to positive and negative SDMs, we have argued that individuals' current goals are related to the goal status represented in these memories (Çili & Stopa, 2015). When individuals think about a positive SDM associated with achieved goals, they may not need to be concerned with achieving goals that require effort and can help them satisfy basic needs (e.g., the need to be effective). Instead, they are free to think about travelling the world or trying new hobbies (i.e., recreation/exploration goals). When they think about a negative SDM, however, they are thinking about a memory related to unsatisfied needs and unattained goals. Consequently, they are more likely to turn their attention to goals related to activities that will require effort on their part, for example in terms of education, career, changing a negative behaviour, or learning new skills. In these cases, we have proposed, the self-images of the failure-associated working self represent a standard in positive feedback loops that the working self goals could try to avoid. The aim of these goals is to increase the discrepancy between individuals' actual state and the failure memory-related standard, which can help individuals compensate for past failures.

Through its dynamic nature and constant adaptation, the working self helps individuals respond to their environment while perceiving a sense of continuity of the self. First, the process through which it is activated, together with the sense of reliving accompanying memory retrieval, contributes to the experience of emotions. Second, its self-images tell us who we are as they remind us of our life story, different aspects of ourselves, past failures or successes, and so on. Finally, its goals guide our behaviour. It is therefore safe to say that the working self is a crucial component of the SMS that helps AM achieve its self and directive functions.

Conclusion

In this chapter, we discussed how AM helps individuals maintain a coherent sense of self while also helping them adapt to their circumstances. We focused particularly on the adaptation process by presenting empirical evidence showing that AM retrieval can have an immediate, transient impact on individuals' affective states, self-perceptions, and behaviour. Drawing on the SMS model, we explained how this process may happen and how it helps AM achieve its self and directive functions. At this point, after reading three chapters delving into the memory-self relationship, clinicians reading this book may be confused – after all, in the Introduction we stated that we wanted to use cognitive, social, and personality psychology literature in order to understand the development and maintenance of psychological disorders. The remainder of the book focuses on this topic. Beginning from the next chapter, we use the theories and research evidence presented in the first three chapters to explore the relevance of the memory-self relationship for psychopathology. Chapter 4 focuses on the relevance of AM for psychological well-being and on the consequences of adverse memories and associated intrusive mental images.

References

Austin, A. & Costabile, K. (2017). Two routes toward optimism: How agentic and communal themes in autobiographical memories guide optimism for the future. *Memory, 25*(10), 1358–1365.

Beike, D. R., Adams, L. P., & Naufel, K. Z. (2010). Closure of autobiographical memories moderates their directive effect on behaviour. *Memory, 18*(1), 40–48.

Beike, D. R., Adams, L. P., & Wirth-Beaumont, E. T. (2007). Incomplete inhibition of emotion in specific autobiographical memories. *Memory, 15*(4), 375–389.

Beike, D. R., Kleinknecht, E., & Wirth-Beaumont, E. T. (2004). How emotional and non-emotional memories define the self. In D. R. Beike, J. M. Lampinen, & D. A. Behrend (Eds.), *The self and memory* (pp. 141–159). New York, NY: Psychology Press.

Beike, D. R. & Wirth-Beaumont, E. T. (2005). Psychological closure as a memory phenomenon. *Memory, 13*(6), 574–593.

Belfi, A. M., Karlan, B., & Tranel, T. (2016). Music evokes vivid autobiographical memories. *Memory, 24*(7), 979–989.

Berntsen, D. & Hall, N. M. (2004). The episodic nature of involuntary autobiographical memories. *Memory & Cognition, 32*(5), 789–803.

Bluck, S., Alea, N., Habermas, T., & Rubin, D. C. (2005). A tale of three functions: The self-reported uses of autobiographical memory. *Social Cognition, 23*(1), 91–117.

Bluck, S. & Habermas, T. (2000). The life story schema. *Motivation and Emotion, 24*(2), 121–147.

Boals, A., Hathaway, L. M., & Rubin, D. C. (2011). The therapeutic effects of completing autobiographical memory questionnaires for positive and negative events: An experimental approach. *Cognitive Therapy and Research, 35*(6), 544–549.

Carver, C. S., Scheier, M. F., & Segerstrom, S. C. (2010). Optimism. *Clinical Psychology Review, 30*(7), 879–889.

Charlesworth, L. A., Allen, R. J., Havelka, J., & Moulin, C. J. A. (2016). Who am I? Autobiographical retrieval improves access to self-concepts. *Memory, 24*(8), 1033–1041.

Cheung, W., Wildschut, T., Sedikides, C., Hepper, E. G., Arndt, J., & Vingerhoets, A. J. J. M. (2013). Back to the future: Nostalgia increases optimism. *Personality and Social Psychology Bulletin, 39*(11), 1484–1496.

Çili, S. & Stopa, L. (2015). The retrieval of self-defining memories is associated with the activation of specific working selves. *Memory, 23*(2), 233–253.

Cockerham, E. S., Çili, S., & Stopa, L. (2016). Investigating the phenomenology of imagery following traumatic burn injuries. *Burns, 42*(4), 853–862.

Conway, M. A. (2005). Memory and the self. *Journal of Memory and Language, 53*(4), 594–628.

Conway, M. A., Meares, K., & Standart, S. (2004). Images and goals. *Memory, 12*(4), 525–531.

Conway, M. A., Singer, J. A., & Tagini, A. (2004). The self and autobiographical memory: Correspondence and coherence. *Social Cognition, 22*(5), 491–529.

del Palacio-Gonzalez, A., Berntsen, D., & Watson, L. A. (2017). Emotional intensity and emotion regulation in response to autobiographical memories during dysphoria. *Cognitive Therapy and Research, 41*(4), 530–542.

Eitam, B. & Higgins, E. T. (2010). Motivation in mental accessibility: Relevance of a representation (ROAR) as a new framework. *Social and Personality Psychology Compass, 4*(10), 951–967.

Eitam, B., Miele, D. B., & Higgins, E. T. (2013). Motivated remembering: Remembering as accessibility and accessibility as motivational relevance. In

D. E. Carlston (Ed.), *The Oxford handbook of social cognition* (pp. 463–475). New York, NY: Oxford University Press.

Fazio, R. H., Effrein, E. A., & Falender, V. J. (1981). Self-perception following social interaction. *Journal of Personality and Social Psychology, 41*, 232–242.

Gadeikis, D., Bos, N., Schweizer, S., Murphy, F., & Dunn, B. (2017). Engaging in an experiential processing mode increases positive emotional response during recall of pleasant autobiographical memories. *Behaviour Research and Therapy, 92*, 68–76.

Gillihan, S. J., Kessler, J., & Farah, M. J. (2007). Memories affect mood: Evidence from covert experimental assignment to positive, neutral, and negative memory recall. *Acta Psychologica, 125*(2), 144–154.

Greenhoot, A. F., Sun, S., Bunnell, S. L., & Lindboe, K. (2013). Making sense of traumatic memories: Memory qualities and psychological symptoms in emerging adults with and without abuse histories. *Memory, 21*(1), 125–142.

Hallford, D. J. & Mellor, D. (2016). Brief reminiscence activities improve state well-being and self-concept in young adults: A randomised controlled experiment. *Memory, 24*(10), 1311–1320.

Hetherington, K. & Moulds, M. L. (2015). Abstract recall of a happy memory to repair sad mood in dysphoria: A possible link to negative cognition. *Memory, 23*(6), 817–828.

Houle, I. & Philippe, F. L. (2017). Need satisfaction in episodic memories impacts mood at retrieval and well-being over time. *Personality and Individual Differences, 105*, 194–199.

Jennings, L. E. & McLean, K. C. (2013). Storying away self-doubt: Can narratives dispel threats to the self? *Journal of Research in Personality, 47*, 317–329.

Joormann, J. & Siemer, M. (2004). Memory accessibility, mood regulation, and dysphoria: Difficulties in repairing sad mood with happy memories? *Journal of Abnormal Psychology, 113*(2), 179–188.

Joormann, J., Siemer, M., & Gotlib, I. H. (2007). Mood regulation in depression: Differential effects of distraction and recall of happy memories on sad mood. *Journal of Abnormal Psychology, 116*(3), 484–490.

Josephson, B. R., Singer, J. A., & Salovey, P. (1996). Mood regulation and memory: Repairing sad moods with happy memories. *Cognition and Emotion, 10*(4), 437–444.

Kunda, Z. & Sanitioso, R. (1989). Motivated changes in the self-concept. *Journal of Experimental Social Psychology, 25*, 272–285.

Lardi, C., D'Argembeau, A., Chanal, J., Ghisletta, P., & Van der Linden, M. (2010). Further characterisation of SDMs in young adults: A study of a Swiss sample. *Memory, 18*(3), 293–309.

Lindeman, M. I., Zengel, B., & Skowronski, J. J. (2017). An exploration of the relationship among valence, fading affect, rehearsal frequency, and memory vividness for past personal events. *Memory, 25*(6), 724–735.

McAdams, D. P. (2013). The psychological self as actor, agent, and author. *Perspectives on Psychological Science, 8*(3), 272–295.

McAdams, D. P. (2015). *The art and science of personality development.* New York, NY: Guilford Press.

Nelis, S., Holmes, E. A., Palmieri, R., Bellelli, G., & Raes, F. (2015). Thinking back about a positive event: The impact of processing style on positive affect. *Frontiers in Psychiatry, 6,* 3.

Öner, S. & Gülgöz, S. (2018). Autobiographical remembering regulates emotions: A functional perspective. *Memory, 26*(1), 15–28.

Pezdek, K. & Salim, R. (2011). Physiological, psychological and behavioural consequences of activating autobiographical memories. *Journal of Experimental Social Psychology, 47,* 1214–1218.

Philippe, F. L., Bouizegarene, N., Guilbault, V., Rajotte, G., & Houle, I. (2015). The chicken or the egg? Systematic investigation of the effect of order of administration of memory questionnaires and well-being scales. *Memory, 23*(7), 1056–1069.

Philippe, F. L., Koestner, R., Lecours, S., Beaulieu-Pelletier, G., & Bois, K. (2011). The role of autobiographical memory networks in the experience of negative emotions: How our remembered past elicits our current feelings. *Emotion,* 11(6), 1279–1290.

Philippot, P., Schaefer, A., & Herbette, G. (2003). Consequences of specific processing of emotional information: Impact of general versus specific autobiographical memory priming on emotion elicitation. *Emotion, 3*(3), 270–283.

Rathbone, C. J. & Moulin, C. J. (2017). Switch costs in the self-memory system. *The Quarterly Journal of Experimental Psychology, 70*(6), 1063–1073.

Ritchie, T. D., Batteson, T. J., Bohn, A., Crawford, M. T., Ferguson, G. V., et al. (2015). A pancultural perspective on the fading affect bias in autobiographical memory. *Memory, 23*(2), 278–290.

Ritchie, T. D., Sedikides, C., & Skowronski, J. J. (2016). Emotions experienced at event recall and the self: Implications for the regulation of self-esteem, self-continuity and meaningfulness. *Memory, 24*(5), 577–591.

Ritchie, T. D., Skowronski, J. J., Cadogan, S., & Sedikides, C. (2014). Affective responses to self-defining autobiographical events. *Self and Identity, 13*(5), 513–534.

Schaefer, A. & Philippot, P. (2005). Selective effects of emotion on the phenomenal characteristics of autobiographical memories. *Memory, 13*(2), 148–160.

Scholer, A. A., Ozaki, Y., & Higgins, E. T. (2014). Inflating and deflating the self: Sustaining motivational concerns through self-evaluation. *Journal of Experimental Social Psychology, 51,* 60–73.

Seebauer, L., Arthen, T., Austermann, M., Falck, J., Koch, L., et al. (2016). Mood repair in healthy individuals: Both processing mode and imagery content matter. *Journal of Behavior Therapy and Experimental Psychiatry, 50,* 289–294.

Selimbegović, L., Régner, I., Huguet, P., & Chatard, A. (2016). On the power of autobiographical memories: From threat and challenge appraisals to actual behaviour. *Memory, 24*(10), 1382–1389.

Selimbegović, L., Régner, I., Sanitioso, R. B., & Huguet, P. (2011). Influence of general and specific autobiographical recall on subsequent behavior: The case of cognitive performance. *Journal of Experimental Social Psychology, 47*, 72–78.

Seto, E., Hicks, J. A., Vess, M., & Geraci, L. (2016). The association between vivid thoughts of death and authenticity. *Motivation and Emotion, 40*(4), 520–540.

Singer, J. A. & Salovey, P. (1993). *The remembered self: Emotion and memory in personality.* New York, NY: The Free Press.

Skowronski, J. J., Walker, W. R., Henderson, D. X., & Bond, G. D. (2014). The fading affect bias: Its history, its implications, and its future. *Advances in Experimental Social Psychology, 49*, 163–218.

Strelan, P. & Zdaniuk, A. (2015). Threatened state self-esteem reduces forgiveness. *Self and Identity, 14*(1), 16–32.

Tsai, W. & Lau, A. S. (2013). Cultural differences in emotion regulation during self-reflection on negative personal experiences. *Cognition and Emotion, 27*(3), 416–429.

Tulving, E. (1985). Memory and consciousness. *Canadian Psychology/Psychologie Canadienne, 26*(1), 1–12.

Tulving, E. (2002). Episodic memory: From mind to brain. *Annual Review of Psychology, 53*(1), 1–25.

Vanderlind, W. M., Stanton, C. H., Weinbrecht, A., Velkoff, E. A., & Joormann, J. (2017). Remembering the good ole days: Fear of positive emotion relates to affect repair using positive memories. *Cognitive Therapy and Research, 41*(3), 362–368.

Walker, W. R., Skowronski, J. J., & Thompson, C. P. (2003). Life is pleasant – and memory helps to keep it that way! *Review of General Psychology, 7*(2), 203–210.

Watson, L. A., Berntsen, D., Kuyken, W., & Watkins, E. R. (2012). The characteristics of involuntary and voluntary autobiographical memories in depressed and never depressed individuals. *Consciousness and Cognition, 21*, 1382–1392.

Werner-Seidler, A. & Moulds, M. L. (2014). Recalling positive self-defining memories in depression: The impact of processing mode. *Memory, 22*(5), 525–535.

Werner-Seidler, A., Tan, L., & Dalgleish, T. (2017). The vicissitudes of positive autobiographical recollection as an emotion regulation strategy in depression. *Clinical Psychological Science, 5*(1), 26–36.

Wheeler, M., Stuss, D., & Tulving, E. (1997). Toward a theory of episodic memory: The frontal lobes and autonoetic consciousness. *Psychological Bulletin, 121*, 331–354.

Wisco, B. E., Marx, B. P., Sloan, D. M., Gorman, K. R., Kulish, A. L., & Pineles, S. L. (2015). Self-distancing from trauma memories reduces physiological but not subjective emotional reactivity among veterans with posttraumatic stress disorder. *Clinical Psychological Science, 3*(6), 956–963.

Zijlema, A., van den Hoven, E., & Eggen, B. (2017). A qualitative exploration of memory cuing by personal items in the home. *Memory Studies.* Advance online publication.

4   Implications of the memory-self relationship for psychological well-being

Introduction

So far, we have presented literature (e.g., Bluck, Alea, Habermas, & Rubin, 2005) suggesting that autobiographical memory (AM) helps individuals develop a sense of self, directs their behaviour, and facilitates interpersonal relationships. Based on this literature, we have argued that by drawing conclusions about the self and learning from their experiences individuals are able to construct a positive, relatively coherent sense of self that facilitates daily functioning. However, individuals can sometimes struggle to construct a positive or coherent life story. They can draw negative conclusions about themselves, other people, or the world from their experiences. They can also experience negative emotions and self-evaluations and engage in dysfunctional behaviours when they recall AMs. Memory, therefore, can have either a beneficial or a detrimental effect.

The aim of the present chapter is to review the existing literature on how AMs contribute to psychological well-being and to the onset and maintenance of psychological disorders. This endeavour is complex because psychological well-being is also influenced by other factors. Furthermore, the evidence on the contribution of AM itself is often inconclusive and sometimes presents methodological issues, including lack of consistency in the assessment of the relevant constructs and the use of cross-sectional designs that make it difficult to determine causality in the relationship between AM and well-being (see Adler, Lodi-Smith, Philippe, & Houle, 2016; Williams et al., 2007). Acknowledging these issues and the fact that this relationship can be reciprocal, we focus on how AM may influence well-being. In the first part of this chapter, we look at how memory features (content, affect, meaning making, and specificity) can shape the memories' self and directive functions and thus influence well-being. In the second part, we discuss the role of intrusive memories and related mental images in psychopathology.

Memory content and affect and psychological well-being

The type of experiences that individuals have and, therefore, the content of their AMs are important for psychological well-being. Adverse experiences (especially those occurring in childhood) can be associated with psychopathology over the lifespan (Clark, Caldwell, Power, & Stansfeld, 2010). In fact, traumatic experiences (e.g., physical, sexual, and psychological abuse) or less severe negative experiences (e.g., parental divorce, being bullied or teased, hospitalisation) are often reported by clinical populations, including patients with social anxiety disorder (Norton & Abbott, 2017), depression and dysthymia (Chapman et al., 2004), body dysmorphic disorder (Buhlmann, Marques, & Wilhelm, 2012; Buhlmann et al., 2011), personality disorders (Lobbestael, Arntz, & Bernstein, 2010), and schizophrenia (Berna et al., 2011; Raffard et al., 2009, 2010). For posttraumatic stress disorder (PTSD), exposure to traumatic events such as serious injury or sexual violence is part of the diagnostic criteria in the *Diagnostic and Statistical Manual of Mental Disorders* (DSM-5; American Psychiatric Association, 2013).

The affect associated with a memory is also relevant for well-being. Overall, research suggests that individuals tend to remember and perceive positive AMs as more central to their identity and life story than negative AMs (e.g., Berntsen, Rubin, & Siegler, 2011; Zaragoza Scherman, Salgado, Shao, & Berntsen, 2015). They also tend to rate the content of their life story chapters as positive (Thomsen, Olesen, Schnieber, & Tønnesvang, 2014). The tendency to retrieve more positive self-defining memories (SDMs) is generally negatively correlated with distress (e.g., anxiety, depression, low self-esteem) (Blagov & Singer, 2004; Nandrino & Gandolphe, 2017). Reporting life story chapters with a positive emotional tone is also related to higher subjective well-being (Pedersen, Staarup, & Thomsen, 2018; Thomsen, Lind, & Pillemer, 2017), higher self-esteem and self-concept clarity (Steiner, Thomsen, & Pillemer, 2017), and lower levels of psychopathology (Holm & Thomsen, 2018). Clinical populations often report more negativity in their memories and life story chapters. Individuals with more depressive symptoms are more likely to retrieve negative turning point (life-changing) memories, whereas individuals experiencing high life satisfaction are more likely to retrieve positive ones (Luchetti, Rossi, Montebarocci, & Sutin, 2016). Patients with schizophrenia often report memories that are less positive (Allé et al., 2015) and less likely to reflect achievement (Raffard et al.,

2009, 2010) than those of healthy individuals. Patients with depression (Dalgleish, Hill, Golden, Morant, & Dunn, 2011), bipolar disorder (Pedersen et al., 2018), and schizophrenia (Holm, Thomsen, & Bliksted, 2016) also tend to describe their life stories as more negative than healthy individuals. Finally, the extent to which individuals perceive adverse memories as central to their identity and life story is negatively associated with well-being and positively associated with depression and PTSD symptoms (Berntsen & Rubin, 2006; Berntsen et al., 2011; Boals, 2010; Zaragoza Scherman et al., 2015).

Meaning making, narrative structure, and psychological well-being

The way in which individuals narrate and make sense of their experiences can have a significant impact on psychological well-being above and beyond individual differences such as personality traits (for a review, see Adler et al., 2016). Existing research in this area focuses on the narrative structure and meanings of unique AMs, life chapters, or the entire life story. Despite methodological differences in the operationalisation and assessment of the different constructs (e.g., well-being), it presents a relatively consistent pattern of findings. In this section, we review these findings by grouping them according to a framework developed by Adler and his colleagues (2016) with the help of narrative identity experts. Specifically, we focus on narratives' motivational themes, affective themes, integrative meaning themes, and structural elements.

Motivational themes. Motivational themes reveal what the individual has sought (and maybe achieved) in the past or is currently seeking (Adler et al., 2016). They are thus related to individuals' goals and refer primarily to agency (e.g., autonomy, achievement) on the one hand and communion (e.g., intimacy, caring) on the other. Overall, research shows that narrating personal experiences with a sense of agency and interpersonal connection tends to be positively associated with well-being (see Adler et al., 2016). It may also support well-being over time. Adler and his colleagues (2015, Study 1) found that a greater sense of agency expressed in different types of memories was associated with a positive mental health trajectory over a 4-year period. This was particularly the case when agency was expressed in negative memories and memories reflecting health challenges. In Study 2, these authors found that participants who developed a major physical illness and had previously reported narratives with higher levels of agency and communion experienced positive mental health trajectories over a 2-year period.

Further research on motivational themes has focused on vulnerable or clinical populations. Adler, Chin, Kolisetty, and Oltmanns (2012) found that themes of agency in the life story and the extent to which memory narratives indicated the satisfaction of communal needs were negatively correlated with borderline personality disorder (BPD) features. The levels of agency reflected in the life story were negatively associated with depression at 6- and 12-month follow-ups. These findings suggest that individuals with BPD features may hold memories of events in which their agentic and communal needs were not met and may reflect the instability of their interpersonal relationships (Adler et al., 2012). In vulnerable populations, however, motivational themes may not always be beneficial. McCoy and Dunlop (2017) compared narratives of different types of memories in adult children of alcoholics and non-alcoholics. They found that the children of alcoholics reported lower levels of agency than their counterparts. Agency in memory narratives was positively associated with emotion dysregulation among children of alcoholics but not among control participants. This suggests that constructing narratives with more perceptions of personal autonomy and control can sometimes be counterproductive (McCoy & Dunlop, 2017). One possible explanation is that perceiving agency is likely to be detrimental when individuals are interpreting an event over which they had no control. For example, trauma survivors with PTSD may demonstrate a high sense of agency and blame the trauma on themselves, even though in reality there was nothing they could have done to prevent or stop it. This may be in order to preserve a sense of control over their life or to adhere to their culture's master narratives, which we discussed in Chapter 2. If master narratives emphasise a sense of agency and personal responsibility, individuals may construct agentic narratives even when this is not warranted.

Affective themes. In Adler et al.'s (2016) framework, affective themes refer to the emotional quality of a narrative. Although they also include narratives' positive or negative emotional tone, in this section we focus only on contamination and redemption sequences. These sequences indicate shifts in the emotional valence of a narrative (from negative to positive in redemption and from positive to negative in contamination), but these shifts may occur as a result of meaning making (see Chapter 2). We thus review redemption and contamination separately from the affect associated with a memory or life story narrative.

The findings on affective themes vary according to the conceptualisation and measurement of well-being, but overall they suggest that both contamination and redemption are associated with well-being (see Adler et al., 2016). Redemption sequences in memory or life story narratives are associated with a positive mental health trajectory over time (Adler et al., 2015), high generativity (McAdams, Reynolds, Lewis, Patten, & Bowman, 2001), high self-esteem (McLean & Breen, 2009), and psychological well-being and adjustment (McAdams et al., 2001; Philippe, Koestner, Beaulieu-Pelletier, & Lecours, 2011; Weststrate & Glück, 2017). Lodi-Smith, Geise, and Roberts (2009) also found that exploratory processing (redemption sequences, narrative coherence, and causal descriptions of change) in students' narratives of personality change during college was associated with increases in emotional health over the previous 4 years. The composite index they created to reflect emotional health comprised self-esteem, life satisfaction, adjustment to college, stress, and depression.

By comparison, contamination sequences are generally related to negative outcomes. They are associated with poor mental health and a negative mental health trajectory over time (Adler et al., 2015), low generativity (McAdams et al., 2001), and depression and low self-esteem (Adler, Kissel, & McAdams, 2006; McAdams et al., 2001). Waters, Shallcross, and Fivush (2013) also found that contamination sequences in memories of intensely negative or traumatic events may be associated with levels of posttraumatic symptoms. In Lodi-Smith et al.'s (2009) longitudinal study, describing the narrative of personality change over a 4-year period as more positive, less negative, and with low levels of contamination was associated with increases in emotional health over time.

However, some studies have failed to find the expected relationship between affective themes and well-being. For example, McCoy and Dunlop (2017) found that redemptive imagery in AMs was positively associated with depression, negative affect, and emotion dysregulation in adult children of alcoholics. There are various possible explanations for this. One possibility is that sometimes participants include in their narratives redemptive statements that they are formulating while retrieving their memories rather than meanings they have reflected about at length (Greenhoot, Sun, Bunnell, & Lindboe, 2013). Another explanation is that sometimes individuals feel pressured to show signs of redemption (McCoy & Dunlop, 2017). As discussed in Chapter 2, redemption narratives are powerful master narratives that dictate how people in Western cultures are expected to interpret and narrate adversity. Even programmes such as Alcoholics Anonymous emphasise redemption as part of recovery, something that individuals with chronic addiction may struggle with because of the repeated adversity they experience (see Singer, 1997). Because of cultural pressures, individuals may feel obliged to show that they are moving on and growing following adverse events, even when this does not reflect their experience. Indicators of redemption in memory narratives, therefore, may not always reflect genuine growth and positive change. This could be why they are sometimes negatively associated with well-being.

Themes of integrative meaning. According to Adler and colleagues (2016), integrative meaning themes represent the extent to which individuals make meaning-related evaluations about a particular memory or about their life story, for example with regards to lessons learnt or to enduring or changed aspects of the self. As these authors conclude, such themes are generally associated with positive outcomes. For example, they have been positively associated with identity development (McLean & Pratt, 2006); self-acceptance, personal growth, and purpose in life (Philippe et al., 2011); and moderate self-restraint (e.g., impulse control, suppression of aggression) (Blagov & Singer, 2004). These findings have important implications for individuals who may struggle to engage in meaning making. For example, patients with schizophrenia tend to report fewer integrative SDMs and less meaning making than healthy controls (Berna et al., 2011; Raffard et al., 2009, 2010). They may be less likely than healthy individuals to identify SDMs as part of life story chapters, possibly because they struggle to locate SDMs in their life story and link them to other memories (Holm et al., 2016). Patients with more negative symptoms (e.g., social isolation, apathy) may make fewer self-event connections in their SDMs (Raffard et al., 2010) and report fewer SDMs, especially SDMs formed after receiving a diagnosis (Holm, Pillemer, Bliksted, & Thomsen, 2017). In these patients, reduced meaning making can be an attempt to protect the self from potentially negative information (Holm et al., 2017). It could also result from impairments in metacognition, the ability to think about one's own and others' thought processes (Holm et al., 2017; Raffard et al., 2009).

Occasionally, integrative meaning is negatively associated with well-being (see Adler et al., 2016). This has been observed, for example, in early adolescents (McLean, Breen, & Fournier, 2010) and African American adolescents coming from challenging low-socioeconomic-status backgrounds (Sales, Merrill, & Fivush, 2013). One explanation for these findings is that meaning making can cause distress in individuals (e.g., adolescents) who lack the cognitive resources needed to process and coherently organise their life experiences or the abstract information acquired from them (see Habermas & Bluck, 2000). It may also be counterproductive for individuals exposed to repeated or prolonged adversity (Sales et al., 2013). Another explanation is that meaning making may be beneficial only over time (see Adler et al., 2016; Park, 2010) and that statements used as evidence of integrative meaning in memory narratives sometimes signal what Park (2010) refers to as *meaning-making efforts* rather than *meaning made*. According to Park, attempts to make meaning may be related to distress and resemble rumination until individuals are able to reduce discrepancies between their beliefs, emotions, and goals, and the challenges posed by a specific experience. Finally, the failure to find a positive relationship between integrative meaning and well-being in some studies may be due to the fact that these studies do not differentiate between meanings. Meaning can be either positive or negative and, according to Pals (2006), individuals need to draw positive meanings and achieve a *coherent positive resolution* in order to reap their benefits. They need to construct a narrative of their experiences (especially of negative ones) that ends positively (i.e., is redemptive) and produces a sense of resolution and being able to move on – at least emotionally. In this way, they can achieve *closure* (Beike, Kleinknecht, & Wirth-Beaumont, 2004), a sense that they have understood the memory and left it behind which is associated with the fading of the memory's affect.

In line with Pals' (2006) argument, research shows that making positive connections between an experience and the self (e.g., in terms of growth) is positively associated with indicators of psychological well-being, whereas making negative connections – especially in narratives of negative memories – is associated with measures of distress (e.g., Banks & Salmon, 2013, 2018; Lilgendahl & McAdams, 2011; Merrill, Waters, & Fivush, 2016). In a recent study, Banks and Salmon (2018) also found that the presence of negative self-event connections in memory narratives was related to rumination and interacted with negative explanatory style (individuals' tendency to attribute negative life events to internal, stable, and global characteristics of the self) in predicting depression. Pedersen and colleagues (2018) found that making more positive connections between life story chapters and the self was related to higher life satisfaction, whereas Holm and Thomsen (2018) found that life story chapter connections indicating more negative self-change or self-stability and connections indicating less positive self-change were related to more severe symptoms of psychopathology. Liao, Bluck, and Westerhof (2018) found that positive meaning making in SDMs and adaptively using SDMs for social, self, and directive functions predicted participants' self-esteem one year later. Pals (2006), on the other hand, found that coherent positive resolution in the narratives of the most challenging and influential life period was associated with more positive outcomes from young adulthood to late midlife. She suggests that coherent positive resolution of challenging experiences may promote enduring positive self-transformation and enhance life satisfaction, whereas unresolved experiences may weaken the self and lead to lingering negative thoughts and emotions.

Although integrative meaning and coherent positive resolution can be beneficial, they may be difficult to achieve in adverse memories. Such memories usually represent challenges to the self, cause disruptions in individuals' lives, and go against the norms prescribed in the cultural life script (Berntsen et al., 2011). As a result, adverse memories may require a greater effort to understand and interpret. In fact, individuals are more likely to report meaning making in adverse memories (e.g., McLean & Pratt, 2006; McLean & Thorne, 2003) and memories that are inconsistent with current self-views (Mutlutürk & Tekcan, 2016). The self-memory system (SMS) model (e.g., Conway, Meares, & Standart, 2004; Conway & Pleydell-Pearce, 2000), together with trauma and PTSD theories (e.g., Ehlers & Clark, 2000; see also Brewin, 2016), agree that negative or traumatic memories threaten the stability of the self because there is a discrepancy between them and individuals' current self-images and goals. In an attempt to maintain self-coherence, the SMS may focus on protecting the self, for example by disrupting the encoding of the experience or distorting the adverse memory in such a way that it fits with current self-views (Conway et al., 2004; Conway & Pleydell-Pearce, 2000). This can happen, for example, when highly autonomous trauma survivors convince themselves that they could have prevented the trauma instead of accepting the fact that some things are beyond their control. Because of the challenges that trauma memories present for the self and the life story, traditional theories (e.g., Conway & Pleydell-Pearce, 2000; Ehlers & Clark, 2000) have stated that these memories may be difficult to integrate with individuals' autobiographical knowledge or sense of self. Of course, integration does occur. Trauma memories can become self-defining (Sutherland & Bryant, 2005) and central to identity and the life story (Berntsen & Rubin, 2006). The fact that the centrality of traumatic events can be associated with negative reactions such as posttraumatic symptoms (Berntsen & Rubin, 2006), however, suggests that integration (at least initially) may involve negative self-trauma connections.

Structural narrative elements. In Adler et al.'s (2016) framework, structural elements indicate how a narrative is told (e.g., in terms of coherence, complexity, and detail). Coherence is assessed through various coding schemes, but it often focuses on aspects such as information about the context of the story, making affective evaluations about the main point of the story, temporal sequencing and narrating the story in such a way that a situation is described and resolved, and integration (the extent to which the story is related to broader life themes and meanings) (e.g., Baerger & McAdams, 1999). As Adler and his colleagues point out, the evidence on the relationship between structural elements and psychological well-being is limited, but it does suggest that individuals experiencing high well-being tend to narrate detailed and coherent stories.

The relationship between narrative structure and well-being, however, seems to be complex. Some studies (e.g., Graci, Watts, & Fivush, 2018; Waters et al., 2013) have found that structural elements (e.g., temporal and thematic coherence) in narratives of various negative events can be related to higher levels of distress, potentially because in these cases individuals make a greater effort to understand the experience and organise the memory (see Graci et al., 2018). In their study of at-risk African American adolescents, Sales et al. (2013) found that self-esteem and depression were not significantly related to temporal coherence, contextual coherence (situating events in time and place), or thematic coherence (staying on topic and elaborating on the events). Their findings suggest that, for vulnerable populations, factors other than coherence may be more important for well-being. Finally, culture may also influence the importance of structural elements. In a study investigating adolescents from Māori, Chinese, and European cultures in New Zealand, Reese and her colleagues (2017) found that thematic coherence was significantly related to life satisfaction only in the Māori sample, potentially because of the importance of memory and narrative in Māori culture.

As some of the above findings suggest, the complexity of the relationship between narrative structure and well-being can be particularly observed in trauma memories. Evidence-based theories of such memories and PTSD (e.g., Brewin, Dalgleish, & Joseph, 1996; Brewin, Gregory, Lipton, & Burgess, 2010; Ehlers & Clark, 2000) argue that during traumatic experiences individuals shift from verbal, contextual processing of information to sensory processing. As a result, the sensory representations of the trauma (e.g., visual images, sounds, smells) may be disconnected from representations of details about the event's context and interpretation. This may result in memories of the trauma that are poorly integrated with their context, disorganised, and fragmented. It may be more common in clinical populations, such as patients with PTSD, who can have vivid recollections of some aspects of the trauma but impaired memory for others (see Brewin, 2007, 2016). Despite these findings, overall the evidence on the coherence and fragmentation of trauma memories and PTSD is inconclusive (see Berntsen &

Rubin, 2014; Brewin, 2016; Crespo & Fernández-Lansac, 2016; Rubin, Berntsen, Ogle, Deffler, & Beckham, 2016).

The evidence on narrative structure in disorders other than PTSD is still limited. Adler et al. (2012) found that narrative coherence in the life story (conceptualised in terms of the presence of context, logical flow, the use of affect-related language to make evaluative points, and integration) was negatively associated with measures of BPD symptoms. Allé and colleagues (2015) found that patients with schizophrenia made fewer statements indicating causal coherence (self-event connections indicating self-change) in the narratives of their most important experiences and life story compared to healthy controls (but see Holm et al., 2016). Patients' life story narratives also demonstrated lower temporal coherence than those of controls. Similarly, Raffard et al. (2010) found that SDM narratives of schizophrenia patients were less coherent (less contextualised, chronologically organised, and developed thematically) than those of control participants.

Memory specificity and psychological well-being

The AM literature distinguishes between specific and non-specific or overgeneral memories. Specific memories refer to unique events that happened within a 24-hour period (Singer & Blagov, 2000; Williams et al., 2007), whereas non-specific memories refer to events that lasted more than 24 hours or that were repeated over time. Specific memories contain significant sensory and spatiotemporal detail if they are self-defining (Singer & Blagov, 2000), although the tendency to retrieve specific memories is not necessarily related to recalling detailed ones (Kyung, Yanes-Lukin, & Roberts, 2016).

The tendency to retrieve overgeneral memories or to report reduced memory specificity is a transdiagnostic factor (Hallford & Mellor, 2017). It is commonly observed in individuals experiencing dysphoria and depression (for reviews, see Dalgleish & Werner-Seidler, 2014; McKay, Castagna, Singer, & Conway, in press; Moore & Zoellner, 2007; Williams et al., 2007) and individuals with, or at risk of developing, bipolar disorder (Dempsey, Gooding, & Jones, 2014; Mansell & Lam, 2004). It may also be present in dissociative identity disorder (Huntjens, Wessel, Hermans, & Van Minnen, 2014); alcohol use disorders (see Nandrino, Gandolphe, & El Haj, 2017); eating disorders (Dalgleish et al., 2003); health-related memories in somatic symptom disorder (Walentynowicz, Raes, Van Diest, & Van den Bergh, 2017); and in avoidant, dependent, and obsessive-compulsive personality disorders (Spinhoven, Bamelis, Molendijk, Haringsma, & Arntz, 2009). Individuals with PTSD can report vivid recollections of their trauma while reporting a bias towards overgeneral retrieval for other memories (Huntjens et al., 2014; see also Moore & Zoellner, 2007). Individuals with BPD may also retrieve overgeneral impoverished memories, but findings are inconsistent and some studies do not find evidence of overgeneral retrieval once they control for levels of depression (for reviews, see Bech, Elklit, & Simonsen, 2015; Van den Broeck, Claes, Pieters, Hermans, & Raes, 2015). Finally, individuals with schizophrenia also tend to display an impaired ability to retrieve specific AMs and to access details from their memories (for reviews, see Berna et al., 2016; Ricarte, Ros, Latorre, & Watkins, 2017). They may, however, be able to retrieve specific SDMs (Raffard et al., 2009, 2010).

Overgeneral retrieval may result from multiple factors. One such factor is exposure to traumatic experiences (Barry, Lenaert, Hermans, Raes, & Griffith, 2018; Moore & Zoellner, 2007). Other factors, which may or may not be related to trauma exposure, are functional avoidance, rumination, and reduced executive resources (Conway & Pleydell-Pearce, 2000; Williams et al., 2007). First, overgeneral retrieval may occur when individuals interrupt the memory search process before they access specific details in order to avoid the negative affect associated with particular AMs. In fact, it is associated with a tendency to avoid negative affect in the face of threatening information or to manage one's emotions by avoiding or ignoring memories (Blagov & Singer, 2004; Harris et al., 2016). Second, rumination may stop the search for specific memories when individuals encounter and then focus their attention on general (usually negative) self-related information. Indeed, there seems to be a relationship between overgeneral retrieval and rumination, and reduced memory specificity may exert an effect on anxiety and depression symptoms through rumination (Hallford & Mellor, 2017; Raes et al., 2006). Low memory specificity can also be related to more perceived permanent change in the self as a result of adverse experiences, and both rumination and perceived permanent change in the self mediate the relationship between overgeneral memory and PTSD and depression in the long run (Kleim & Ehlers, 2008). Finally, overgeneral retrieval may occur when individuals have few cognitive resources available for AM searches during voluntary retrieval, for example because of working memory issues or an impaired ability to filter out irrelevant information. This may account for overgeneral retrieval in disorders characterised by significant dysfunction, such as schizophrenia (Berna et al., 2016) or alcohol use disorders (Nandrino et al., 2017).

Despite the growing evidence, our understanding of the involvement of avoidance, rumination, and reduced executive resources in the disorders characterised by overgeneral retrieval is still limited. Williams and colleagues (2007), however, propose that these processes may operate simultaneously. For example, following a traumatic event, an individual may experience intrusive trauma-related mental images and ruminate about the trauma. Added to constant attempts to avoid the trauma memory, this may lead to reduced cognitive resources and stop memory search processes before specific memory details can be accessed. Over time, what can start as a defence against the trauma memory may expand to other memories (even positive ones), with overgeneral retrieval becoming the individual's habitual method of retrieval (Singer, Blagov, Berry, & Oost, 2013; Williams et al., 2007).

Understanding the influence of AMs on well-being through their characteristics and functions

The literature presented so far in this chapter suggests that the characteristics of memories and how individuals remember, interpret, and narrate these memories have important implications for psychological well-being. At this point, the evidence on the exact ways in which memory or retrieval characteristics influence well-being – either individually or by interacting with each other and with individual differences – is still limited. However, in this section we bring together the existing memory and clinical literature in order to understand some of the processes involved. We propose that understanding how AMs contribute to well-being requires an appreciation of the influence that different memory characteristics have on the overall memory-self relationship and on the way in which memories perform their self and directive functions. We consider these two functions separately, but we acknowledge that they overlap and are difficult to tease apart (see Harris, Rasmussen, & Berntsen, 2014).

Memory characteristics and the self function of AM. As mentioned in Chapter 2, individuals are motivated to maintain a positive sense of self, as well as feelings of self-continuity, unity, and purpose (e.g., McAdams, 2015). They use AMs strategically to achieve this aim (see Sedikides, Green, & Pinter, 2004; Wilson & Ross, 2003). Current evidence suggests that this process depends on memory characteristics. Content and affect, for example, may help establish and maintain a positive view of the self. Individuals with high self-esteem are more likely than individuals with low self-esteem to report positive SDMs (D'Argembeau, Lardi, & Van der Linden, 2012). This relationship may be partly due to the association between AMs, goal attainment, and need satisfaction (see

Chapters 2 and 3). Holding memories indicating need satisfaction can in fact be positively related to well-being (Lekes, Guilbault, Philippe, & Houle, 2014; Philippe et al., 2011). Furthermore, since memories may affect state self-esteem when they are retrieved (Çili & Stopa, 2015a), it is possible that repeated activation of positive memories may contribute to increases in trait self-esteem. Negative memories, on the other hand, may trigger negative self-evaluations upon retrieval and remind individuals of failure and thwarted needs. Their frequent activation may be associated with low self-esteem, which could become chronic over time. In the long run, changes to self-esteem could affect well-being. In fact, self-esteem is positively related to psychological well-being (e.g., Paradise & Kernis, 2002).

Meaning making can help individuals achieve not only a positive view of the self, but also a sense of unity and purpose (see Adler et al., 2016; Habermas & Bluck, 2000; McAdams, 2015). Interpretations that involve positive self-event connections, coherent positive resolution, and perceptions of agency and communion can enhance self-esteem. Furthermore, as discussed in Chapter 2, meaning making and constructing coherent narratives help individuals link the past, present, and the future and thus establish a sense of self-continuity. This argument is supported by Habermas and Köber (2015), who found that autobiographical reasoning was positively associated with perceptions of self-continuity when individuals had experienced disruptive life experiences. Holm and Thomsen (2018) also found that higher self-concept clarity was related to higher ratings of positive and lower ratings of negative self-event connections and emotional tone in life story chapters. Self-concept clarity refers to the extent to which the contents of an individual's self-concept are "clearly and confidently defined, internally consistent, and temporally stable" and may thus indicate self unity and continuity (Campbell, Assanand, & Di Paula, 2003; Campbell et al., 1996, p. 141). It is positively related to self-esteem (Campbell et al., 1996) and psychological adjustment (Bigler, Neimeyer, & Brown, 2001; Campbell et al., 2003), and may be low in individuals experiencing psychological issues. Stopa, Brown, Luke, and Hirsch (2010), for example, found that self-concept clarity predicts social anxiety, with high socially anxious individuals reporting lower clarity than low socially anxious ones.

Establishing self-continuity does not mean focusing only on past and present selves. As mentioned in Chapter 2, individuals can hold imagined representations of the self and future events. Meaning making can give rise to new self-images; goals; and self-defining future projections (SDFPs), which are representations of future events that shape current and future views of the self and that are constructed and interpreted in the same way as SDMs (D'Argembeau et al., 2012). It may thus help project individuals into a future that is usually perceived as positive and filled with achievements (D'Argembeau et al., 2012; Thomsen et al., 2014). Both thinking about SDMs and imagining future events can actually be associated with a sense of self-continuity and contribute to self-esteem (D'Argembeau et al., 2012; Demblon & D'Argembeau, 2017). This suggests that future projections are important for well-being. In fact, individuals with remitted bipolar disorder generate fewer future life story chapters and struggle to imagine a distant future compared to non-clinical controls (Pedersen et al., 2018). Individuals with schizophrenia, who experience disturbances in their sense of self, find it difficult to engage in meaning making for SDFPs and report that SDFPs give them a lower sense of self-continuity compared to healthy individuals (Raffard et al., 2016).

Finally, overgeneral retrieval may affect the self by preventing individuals from taking full advantage of the cognitive and affective detail contained in specific memories (Singer et al., 2013). For example, the inability to access specific positive memories may prevent individuals from maintaining a positive view of themselves (see Hitchcock, Rees, & Dalgleish, 2017). An inability to access specific, vivid details of the past may also create problems for establishing a sense of self-continuity and could be one of the factors contributing to self-continuity deficits in disorders such as schizophrenia (see Berna et al., 2016). At the same time, overgeneral retrieval and the associated rumination may prevent the updating of the meanings attributed to experiences, thus potentially maintaining negative interpretations of these experiences and contributing to symptoms of psychological disorders (Kleim & Ehlers, 2008; William et al., 2007). If an individual has concluded that they are inadequate after being publicly humiliated and avoids thinking about this experience in specific terms, they may struggle to re-start the meaning making process. The belief about inadequacy may distort their recollection of the event and, if they are unable to access the details of what happened, they cannot challenge this belief or make benign connections between the event and their sense of self. Instead, they might attempt to establish thematic and causal coherence in their life story based on this belief. They can re-interpret past experiences or interpret new experiences in light of the belief and see them as evidence confirming it. As a result, the details of these other experiences may become irrelevant and they, too, may be subsequently retrieved in an overgeneral manner.

Memory characteristics and the directive function of AM. Memory characteristics can also affect the way in which AMs perform their directive function. They can do so by influencing individuals' goals and behaviour. The affect and level of need satisfaction associated with a memory may influence the memory's directive function in two main ways. First, it may influence levels of optimism. Moffitt and Singer (1994) found that participants who recalled more positive and less negative SDMs were more optimistic about achieving their goals, whereas those who recalled SDMs with a more negative emotional tone rated goal attainment as more difficult. This is important because how positive individuals feel about achieving specific goals might determine whether they engage in goal-directed behaviours or not. Second, affect can directly influence behaviour. AM activation may be associated with repeated activation of related working selves (self-representations that are active at any one time) and of the level of need satisfaction represented by these AMs (see Chapter 3). Frequent activation of AMs might make the emotions they trigger chronic and lead to enduring changes in well-being (Houle & Philippe, 2017; Philippe & Bernard-Desrosiers, 2017). It could do so partly because of the impact of affect on behaviour. Positive affect is generally associated with a more global processing style (seeing the bigger picture) and promotes flexibility, consideration of a broader pool of alternatives, and more efficient behaviour and problem solving (see Fredrickson, 2001; Isbell & Lair, 2013; Isen, 2004). On the other hand, negative affect can direct individuals' attention towards very specific information, impair decision making, and trigger behaviours that are narrow in scope (see Fredrickson, 2001; Isbell & Lair, 2013; Remmers & Zander, 2018). Need satisfying memories may thus elicit positive, efficient behaviours aimed at achieving growth, whereas memories associated with failure and thwarted needs may signal a threat to the self and elicit self-protective behaviours (Houle & Philippe, 2017; Philippe et al., 2011). In the long run, frequently experienced positive emotions may promote resilience and a broader way of thinking, whereas negative emotions may contribute to psychopathology (Fredrickson, 2001). Repeated experiences of negative affect followed by inefficient decision making and failure to achieve goals, for example, may amplify negative emotions and strengthen negative beliefs about the self.

Meaning making can affect behaviour by influencing goal setting. First, the way in which individuals interpret their experiences, particularly as they establish thematic and causal coherence in their life story, can determine the kind of goals they set (see Bluck & Habermas, 2000). For example, if an individual concludes that they are vulnerable following a traumatic event, they may set trauma-related goals such as *"I want to be safe again."* Such beliefs are commonly reported by patients with PTSD (Huntjens et al., 2016; Sutherland & Bryant, 2005). For these patients, the trauma-relatedness of personal goals can be associated with posttraumatic symptoms (Huntjens et al., 2016). One explanation for this is that goals derived from memories associated with negative self-event connections may not be realistic. Another possibility is that they may trigger maladaptive behaviours which then maintain symptoms. PTSD patients, for example, often try to protect themselves by avoiding trauma reminders, the trauma memory, and situations they perceive as dangerous. In the long run, this avoidance can prevent them from updating the negative beliefs associated with the trauma and limit their exposure to experiences that disconfirm these beliefs (see Ehlers & Clark, 2000).

Overgeneral retrieval can also influence the way in which AM performs its directive function. A person who is unable to access specific positive memories may have reduced opportunities for repairing their mood (see Werner-Seidler & Moulds, 2011) and experiencing positive affect (McKay et al., in press), which can have a beneficial impact on behaviour and problem solving. Furthermore, the inability to access details related to one's past may affect the amount of information that is available during decision making and goal pursuit. As mentioned in Chapter 2, one of the key reasons for retaining goal-relevant memories is that they can inform us of past successful and unsuccessful goal pursuit strategies and lessons learnt. Specific AMs may thus be more efficient than overgeneral ones in supporting goal pursuits and in informing individuals about the probability of reaching a desired outcome (Blagov & Singer, 2004; Singer et al., 2013). In fact, overgeneral memory has been associated with problem solving deficits in clinical populations, including patients with depression (Goddard, Dritschel, & Burton, 1996), remitted bipolar disorder (Scott, Stanton, Garland, & Ferrier, 2000), and BPD (especially when patients are also depressed) (Maurex et al., 2010). On the other hand, instructing individuals to retrieve specific AMs may enable them to recognise and retrieve memories that are helpful for solving interpersonal problems (Goddard, Dritschel, & Burton, 2001). Getting them to think about recent memories in a specific, detailed manner can also enable them to generate more alternative positive outcomes to anticipated negative future events, which may then make them perceive these events as less plausible and less negative (see Jing, Madore, & Schacter, 2017). This can help individuals imagine a more positive future.

Projection into the future is indeed another way in which overgeneral retrieval can influence behaviour. Remembering the past and imagining the future have common cognitive and neural bases and the ability to imagine future events is thought to rely on being able to recombine elements of past AMs (Eustache, Viard, & Desgranges, 2016; Schacter et al., 2012). Indeed, difficulties in remembering the past may be associated with deficits in future thinking (see Szpunar, 2010) and individuals construct SDMs and future events in a similar manner when it comes to specificity (D'Argembeau et al., 2012). This means that an overgeneral retrieval of past memories may translate into overgeneral images of the future. In fact, patients with depression, bipolar disorder, and schizophrenia – who are likely to experience overgeneral retrieval – tend to report less detailed and less specific episodic future thinking than control groups (for a review, see Hallford, Austin, Takano, & Raes, 2018). Reduced specificity and impairments in future thinking have also been observed in BPD, eating disorders (Rasmussen et al., 2017), and alcohol use disorders (Nandrino et al., 2017). Individuals with PTSD (Kleim, Graham, Fihosy, Stott, & Ehlers, 2014), schizophrenia (Raffard, Esposito, Boulenger, & Van der Linden, 2013), depression, and anxiety disorders (Morina, Deeprose, Pusowski, Schmid, & Holmes, 2011) may particularly struggle to imagine vivid and specific *positive* future events. Such difficulties in imagining the future (especially a positive one) can impair individuals' ability to plan ahead, regulate their emotions, and engage in adaptive problem solving and goal-directed behaviours that favour long-term rewards (see Schacter et al., 2012; Szpunar, 2010). A clear illustration of this is the case of schizophrenia, in which an impaired ability to imagine specific future events is associated with apathy, suggesting motivation deficits when it comes to pursuing goals (Raffard et al., 2013).

Summary. In this section, we proposed that memory characteristics can influence how memories perform their self and directive functions, which in turn can influence psychological well-being. The affect associated with AMs and the extent to which AMs reflect goal attainment or need satisfaction may influence self-esteem. It may also become chronic and influence individuals' behaviour and optimism about achieving their goals. Meaning making can influence self-esteem and self-concept clarity as it facilitates the construction of past-, present-, and future-oriented self-images. It can also influence behaviour through lesson learning and goal setting. Finally, memory specificity provides a rich pool of information that individuals can use to construct a positive and continuous sense of self, guide their behaviour, and plan for the future. So far, we have focused primarily on research investigating voluntarily retrieved AMs. However, AMs and related images can also be detrimental to well-being when they are involuntary and intrusive. In the remainder of this chapter, we focus on intrusive AMs and images and on how they contribute to psychological disorders by performing maladaptive self and directive functions.

Intrusive AMs and mental images in psychological disorders

Introduction to intrusive AMs and mental imagery. Involuntary memories, which are experienced in the absence of deliberate attempts at retrieval, are a common element of our conscious experience (Rasmussen & Berntsen, 2011). Occasionally, these memories or images associated with them become highly intrusive and distressing. Mental images are cognitive representations which contain sensory qualities and create the subjective experience of perceiving with the mind's senses, despite arising in the absence of external sensory input (Kosslyn, Ganis, & Thompson, 2001). In PTSD, acute stress disorder, and obsessive-compulsive disorder (OCD), the presence of intrusive and distressing memories or images constitutes a DSM-5 diagnostic criterion (American Psychiatric Association, 2013). Intrusive mental imagery, however, is a transdiagnostic factor (Brewin et al., 2010).

The intrusions reported by individuals with psychological disorders tend to be vivid and recurrent (for reviews, see Brewin et al., 2010; Çili & Stopa, 2015b; Holmes & Mathews, 2010). Their content varies according to the disorder and often matches patients' verbal cognitions and fears (see Table 4.1). They mostly consist of visual elements, but other sensory modalities can also be present. For example, patients with bulimia nervosa may experience food smells and tastes, cutaneous sensations (e.g., clothes feeling tight around the body), and organic elements (e.g., sense of heaviness) (Hinrichsen, Morrison, Waller, & Schmidt, 2007; Somerville, Cooper, & Hackmann, 2007). Patients with a specific phobia of vomiting may experience intrusive images that include physical sensations (e.g., feeling sick), tastes (e.g., taste of recently consumed food), and smells and sounds related to vomiting (Price, Veale, & Brewin, 2012).

Patients experience intrusive images from different perspectives. Patients with disorders like depression (see Holmes, Blackwell, Burnett Heyes, Renner, & Raes, 2016), bulimia nervosa (Somerville et al., 2007), social anxiety disorder (e.g., Wells, Clark, & Ahmad, 1998), and body dysmorphic disorder (Osman et al., 2004) tend to see themselves from an observer perspective (from the outside in). Patients with disorders like OCD (Lipton et al., 2010; Speckens et al., 2007) or specific phobia of vomiting (Price et al., 2012), on the other hand, tend to

Table 4.1 Content of Intrusions in Psychological Disorders

Disorder	Examples of Intrusive Memory / Image Content
Agoraphobia	Physical or mental catastrophes, disorientation, lack of resources to cope with agoraphobic situations, panic (e.g., fainting while crossing the road) (Day, Holmes, & Hackmann, 2004; Hackmann, Day, & Holmes, 2009)
Specific phobia of vomiting	Past memories or imagined worst case scenarios involving the self or others vomiting (Price et al., 2012)
Social anxiety disorder	Worst fears about one's behaviour in social situations being realised (e.g., blushing intensely, making a fool of oneself) (Hackmann, Clark, & McManus, 2000; Hackmann, Surawy, & Clark, 1998)
Obsessive-compulsive disorder	Images depicting unacceptable ideas of harm (e.g., inappropriate aggressive or sexual acts), contamination (e.g., seeing the self covered in faeces or washing thoroughly), and social rejection (Coughtrey, Shafran, & Rachman, 2013, 2015; Lipton, Brewin, Linke, & Halperin, 2010; Speckens, Hackmann, Ehlers, & Cuthbert, 2007)
Body dysmorphic disorder	Exaggerated pictures of and sensations such as tingling in the body parts of concern (Osman, Cooper, Hackmann, & Veale, 2004)
Health anxiety (illness anxiety disorder)	Memories or images related to themes such as receiving the news of having a serious illness, suffering from a serious illness, death (e.g., being accidentally cremated alive), and the impact of one's illness or death on others (Muse, McManus, Hackmann, Williams, & Williams, 2010; Wells & Hackmann, 1993)
Posttraumatic stress disorder	Brief sensory fragments of the trauma signalling its worst moments (Grey & Holmes, 2008) or a shift for the worse in the meaning of this event (Ehlers et al., 2002); non-veridical images, for example related to out-of-body experiences, worst case scenarios (see Grey, 2009), or the afterlife (Wade et al., 2015)
Depression	Past experiences such as own or significant other's illness or injury, threatened or actual assault, and interpersonal problems (Patel et al., 2007; Reynolds & Brewin, 1999; Weßlau, Lieberz, Oertel-Knöchel, & Steil, 2016); flash-forwards to future suicidal behaviour (e.g., jumping in front of a train) (Crane, Shah, Barnhofer, & Holmes, 2012; Holmes, Crane, Fennell, & Williams, 2007)

(continued)

Table 4.1 (Cont.)

Disorder	Examples of Intrusive Memory / Image Content
Bipolar disorder	Negative experiences related to themes such as isolation and victimisation (e.g., interpersonal problems, abuse) and positive events (e.g., winning an award) or positive interactions with others; flash-forwards such as suicide plans (Di Simplicio et al., 2016; Gregory, Brewin, Mansell, & Donaldson, 2010; Mansell & Hodson, 2009)
Bulimia nervosa	Pictures of the self bingeing or vomiting, images of the self as overweight and unattractive, sensations such as clothes being tight or feeling bloated (Hinrichsen et al., 2007; Somerville et al., 2007); images related to food or experiences of social rejection (see Dugué, Keller, Tuschen-Caffier, & Jacob, 2016)
Psychosis	Traumatic experiences (e.g., being assaulted), feared events related to paranoia or persecutory delusions (e.g., being pushed into an oven), perceived sources of auditory hallucinations (e.g., spirits of friends), content of auditory hallucinations (e.g., stabbing someone) (Morrison et al., 2002; Schulze, Freeman, Green, & Kuipers, 2013)

Note. Adapted from *Understanding cognitive changes in imagery rescripting: The role of the memory-imagery-self relationship* (Unpublished doctoral dissertation) (p. 21), by S. Çili, 2012, University of Southampton, United Kingdom. Copyright 2012 by S. Çili.

see themselves from a field perspective (i.e., as if seeing through their own eyes). Imagery perspective can affect the impact of the images on emotions and behaviour. The field perspective generally allows greater engagement with the image and thus produces a more intense emotional response (see Holmes & Mathews, 2010). By comparison, the observer perspective helps individuals to experience the images as detached observers and can reduce the distress associated with them (see Eich, Handy, Holmes, Lerner, & McIsaac, 2011; Holmes & Mathews, 2010). It can also exert a stronger influence on behaviour because it is associated with different perceptions of its causes; compared to the field perspective, the observer perspective can make individuals perceive outcomes as a function of their own actions rather than of situational factors (Libby, Shaeffer, Eibach, & Slemmer, 2007).

Intrusions are usually triggered by environmental or internal stimuli. Patients with social anxiety disorder experience images of the self before, during, or after anxiety-provoking social situations (Clark & Wells, 1995;

Hackmann et al., 2000). Bulimic patients often do so when they worry about their eating, shape, or weight (Somerville et al., 2007) or after binge eating (Hinrichsen et al., 2007). In patients with PTSD, intrusions are often triggered by trauma-related cues, such as objects seen before or during the trauma or emotions and physical sensations experienced around the same time (see Ehlers & Clark, 2000). For individuals who have sustained physical scars (e.g., burn scars) following a traumatic experience, the scars themselves can be powerful triggers for intrusive images related to this experience (Cockerham, Çili, & Stopa, 2016).

Origin of intrusive images. As Table 4.1 shows, sometimes intrusive images can be (at least in part) products of individuals' imagination. In suicidal patients, for example, images may be flash-forwards to future suicidal behaviour or one's funeral (Crane et al., 2012; Holmes et al., 2007; Ng, Di Simplicio, McManus, Kennerley, & Holmes, 2016). In PTSD, they may include composite images from different events (e.g., repeated traumas), worst case scenarios of what could have happened during the trauma, or out-of-body experiences (Grey, 2009). Although such non-veridical images are common, many patients report that their intrusions are related to and resemble memories of adverse experiences in terms of themes, sensory modalities, and emotional tone (e.g., Hackmann et al., 2000; Osman et al., 2004; Somerville et al., 2007).

The memories that give rise to intrusive images tend to be similar across disorders. The images experienced by patients with agoraphobia (Day et al., 2004), OCD (Speckens et al., 2007), health anxiety (Wells & Hackmann, 1993), and bipolar disorder (Tzemou & Birchwood, 2007) are often associated with neglect and physical, psychological, and sexual abuse. Patients with psychosis report intrusions related to experiences involving threat or harm, humiliation, and hospitalisations (Morrison et al., 2002; Schulze et al., 2013). In body dysmorphic disorder, the memories involve being teased or bullied at school and being conscious about physical changes in adolescence (Osman et al., 2004). In depression, they often involve interpersonal problems such as intimate relationship breakdowns (Patel et al., 2007). In bulimia, the memories are related to being humiliated, abused, or abandoned (Hinrichsen et al., 2007); others making negative comments about one's weight/shape; and being conscious about one's appearance (Somerville et al., 2007). In social anxiety disorder, the memories frequently depict experiences of being criticised or bullied, as well as others demonstrating a lack of interest or pointing out an anxiety symptom (Hackmann et al., 2000). Negative social experiences are also linked to intrusions in agoraphobia (Day et al., 2004), health anxiety (Wells & Hackmann, 1993), bipolar disorder (Mansell & Lam, 2004), and OCD (Speckens et al., 2007).

Relationships among intrusive images, negative beliefs, and affect. Intrusions often involve images of the self and incorporate meanings derived from the original memory or appraisals of the intrusions themselves. These meanings are usually negative beliefs about the self, others, and the world. Beliefs about the self sometimes revolve around issues of inadequacy and worthlessness. In health anxiety (Wells & Hackmann, 1993), OCD (Speckens et al., 2007), and psychosis (Morrison et al., 2002), for example, beliefs associated with intrusions include *"I am bad / a failure."* In psychosis, they include *"I deserve to be punished"* (Morrison et al., 2002) and *"I am weak"* (Schulze et al., 2013). Beliefs about others often revolve around trust. Patients suffering from psychosis, for example, may associate their intrusions with beliefs such as *"People cannot be trusted / are out to harm me"* (Morrison et al., 2002; Schulze et al., 2013). Finally, beliefs about the world tend to emphasise injustice or danger. Patients with psychosis (Schulze et al., 2013) and agoraphobia (Hackmann et al., 2009) report beliefs such as *"The world is unjust / unsafe."*

Intrusive images are also associated with a range of negative emotions such as fear, anxiety, helplessness, anger, sadness, and shame (e.g., Gregory et al., 2010; Hackmann et al., 2009; Reynolds & Brewin, 1999; Schulze et al., 2013; Speckens et al., 2007). They may also be associated with emotions related to disorder-specific symptoms. For example, in obsessive-compulsive patients with contamination fears, distressing images may be related to disgust (Speckens et al., 2007). In agoraphobic patients, they are sometimes associated with feeling overwhelmed (Hackmann et al., 2009). In any case, the emotions elicited by intrusive images tend to be intense. This is related to mental images' ability to directly influence the brain's emotional system, their reliance on the same neural structures as perception and subsequent similarity to perceptual experience, and their association with AMs (see Holmes & Mathews, 2010; Pearson, Naselaris, Holmes, & Kosslyn, 2015). In fact, partly because of their relationship with AMs, intrusive images are often accompanied by a sense of reliving the original experiences (see Brewin et al., 2010). This is clearly illustrated in a book titled *Aftershock: The Untold Story of Surviving Peace*, in which journalist Mathew Green (2015) describes the experiences and posttraumatic reactions of military personnel who have served in different conflicts. In describing the sense of reliving accompanying his images, a veteran of the Northern Ireland conflict states, "I am still back in '92, '93, '94. I'm a young, fit soldier again. People are trying to tell me it's 2013 and I'm like: 'You're... lying, you're playing with my head, you're messing about with me.'" (Green, 2015, p. 217). For him and other veterans mentioned in the book, the intrusions have a strong affective impact and powerfully recreate the experience of being back in combat.

Role of images in disorder onset and maintenance. Intrusive images are involved in the onset and maintenance of psychological disorders. Studies focusing on health anxiety (Muse et al., 2010), agoraphobia (Day et al., 2004), body dysmorphic disorder (Osman et al., 2004), and social anxiety disorder (Hackmann et al., 2000) suggest that patients' symptoms either appeared or worsened after they experienced the intrusion-related event. Other studies have linked symptoms with the presence of intrusive images. Distraction by and controllability of mental images of food can be associated with the severity of eating pathology in individuals engaging in binge eating (Dugué et al., 2016). Among socially anxious individuals, levels of distress are associated with the frequency of intrusions and the presence of intrusions is associated with greater anxiety (Homer & Deeprose, 2017). In patients with bipolar disorder, depression may be associated with how demotivating significant intrusive images are at times of low mood (Di Simplicio et al., 2016). Depression is related to the frequency of and distress associated with intrusive AMs and images, with maladaptive AM appraisals, and with intrusion rumination and avoidance (Mihailova & Jobson, 2018). Patients with psychosis and persecutory delusions who experience intrusive images may experience higher levels of delusional distress than patients who do not experience such images (Schulze et al., 2013).

The relationship between intrusions and symptoms may account for the role that intrusions play in disorder maintenance. The experimental evidence on this role is still limited. Some of the experiments conducted to date and evidence from patient interviews suggest that intrusions may contribute to maintenance through the affective and behavioural responses they elicit. For example, in social anxiety disorder, images experienced in social situations may elicit intense anxiety, negative thoughts, and behavioural responses (e.g., safety behaviours such as gaze avoidance), which have a negative impact on patients' performance and make them appear aloof (Clark & Wells, 1995; Ng, Abbott, & Hunt, 2014; see also Norton & Abbott, 2017). In health anxiety, intrusive images can trigger behaviours such as reassurance seeking and body checking. which can help maintain the anxiety (Muse et al., 2010). In bipolar disorder, mental imagery can amplify positive and negative emotions and thus contribute to patients' unstable mood (Holmes, Geddes, Colom, & Goodwin, 2008; O'Donnell, Di Simplicio, Brown, Holmes, & Burnett Heyes, 2017). In OCD, images can trigger anxiety with which patients try to cope by engaging in compulsive behaviours such as washing or checking (see Coughtrey et al., 2013, 2015; Speckens et al., 2007). In bulimia nervosa, mental images (e.g., of food or social rejection) may be associated with an increased desire to eat (see Dugué et al., 2016), but then the self-images and negative emotions elicited after a bingeing episode can trigger self-induced vomiting (Hinrichsen et al., 2007). In PTSD, intrusions and the accompanying sense of reliving often lead to a sense of impending threat and behaviours such as avoidance, thus preventing the disconfirmation of patients' fears and maintaining symptoms (Ehlers & Clark, 2000).

The exact mechanisms through which intrusive images contribute to psychopathology are not yet clear. We have proposed that we can begin to understand them by relying on the SMS model (Çili & Stopa, 2015a, 2015b). According to this model, working selves associated with adverse memories tend to be more easily accessible because these memories threaten the attainment of individuals' goals and therefore may not be integrated or compatible with the long-term self (Conway et al., 2004). Mental images may represent or form part of working selves that are related to the adverse experiences from which they originated (Çili & Stopa, 2015a; Stopa, 2009). As discussed in Chapters 2 and 3, working self goals are involved in positive and negative feedback loops which elicit behaviours aimed at increasing or decreasing the discrepancy between the individual's actual state and a particular standard. Negative intrusive self-images may represent a standard that the self has to avoid in positive feedback loops (Conway et al., 2004). When the working selves associated with them are activated, they can thus trigger negative affect and promote maladaptive behaviours that aim to distance the patient from what they represent. If the intrusive image experienced by a patient with bulimia nervosa after bingeing features her as overweight, it can elicit negative affect and lead to self-induced vomiting which she thinks can prevent her from becoming the person in the image (see Hinrichsen et al., 2007).

Our arguments are partly supported by studies involving imagery manipulation in non-clinical samples. In a sample of students who scored high in body dissatisfaction, Farrar, Stopa, and Turner (2015) found that holding negative body-related self-images in mind led to increased negative affect and reduced positive affect, self-esteem, self-concept clarity, and body satisfaction. Positive self-images had the opposite effect on positive affect, self-esteem, and body satisfaction. Using a similar methodology, Bullock, Newman-Taylor, and Stopa (2016) asked students high in paranoia to recall and hold in mind images related to a situation in which they had felt secure and trusting or a situation in which they had felt suspicious. They found that paranoia-related imagery led to increases in paranoia and negative affect and decreases in positive affect, self-esteem, and self-compassion. Trust-related imagery led to decreases in paranoia and increases in positive affect, self-esteem, and self-compassion.

The above findings illustrate the impact that mental images have on affect and self-perceptions. Together with the evidence reviewed earlier, they suggest that intrusive images related to adverse experiences can fulfil self and directive functions just like voluntarily retrieved AMs. Through representations of the self and encapsulated beliefs potentially representing self-event connections produced through autobiographical reasoning, they can inform individuals about who they are or may become. In addition, they can elicit maladaptive behaviours. Further experimental work is needed to support our arguments. Nevertheless, the existing literature does suggest that the relationship between intrusive images and the self may be the key to understanding their role in psychological disorders.

Conclusion

In this chapter, we discussed the impact of AM on psychological well-being. We focused on how memory characteristics affect the way in which AMs perform their self and directive functions and thus influence well-being. We also argued that AMs may contribute to psychopathology through intrusive mental images. Overall, evidence suggests that a healthy narrative identity and memory system involve the ability to access specific AMs which have a positive affective tone and from which individuals have drawn positive adaptive meanings about the self, others, and the world (McKay et al., in press; Singer et al., 2013). However, individuals do not have complete control over the kind of experiences they are exposed to and do not always succeed in interpreting their experiences positively. When psychological issues arise following particular life experiences, therapeutic interventions may be needed. A major family of therapies that address AMs and related meanings is cognitive-behavioural therapy. Chapter 5 focuses on cognitive-behavioural interventions targeting the self and AM, and identifies ways in which these interventions may benefit from the literature on the memory-self relationship.

Authors' Note

The section on intrusive mental images in this chapter is partially based on Çili (2012) and Çili and Stopa (2015b).

References

Adler, J. M., Chin, E. D., Kolisetty, A. P., & Oltmanns, T. F. (2012). The distinguishing characteristics of narrative identity in adults with features of borderline personality disorder: An empirical investigation. *Journal of Personality Disorders, 26*(4), 498–512.

Adler, J. M., Kissel, E. C., & McAdams, D. P. (2006). Emerging from the CAVE: Attributional style and the narrative study of identity in midlife adults. *Cognitive Therapy and Research, 30*(1), 39–51.

Adler, J. M., Lodi-Smith, J., Philippe, F. L., & Houle, I. (2016). The incremental validity of narrative identity in predicting well-being: A review of the field and recommendations for the future. *Personality and Social Psychology Review, 20*(2), 142–175.

Adler, J. M., Turner, A. F., Brookshier, K. M., Monahan, C., Walder-Biesanz, I., et al. (2015). Variation in narrative identity is associated with trajectories of mental health over several years. *Journal of Personality and Social Psychology, 108*(3), 476–496.

Allé, M. C., Potheegadoo, J., Köber, C., Schneider, P., Coutelle, R., et al. (2015). Impaired coherence of life narratives of patients with schizophrenia. *Nature Scientific Reports, 5*: 12934.

American Psychiatric Association (2013). *Diagnostic and statistical manual of mental disorders (5th ed.)*. Washington, DC: American Psychiatric Publishing.

Baerger, D. R. & McAdams, D. P. (1999). Life story coherence and its relation to psychological well-being. *Narrative Inquiry, 9*, 69–96.

Banks, M. V. & Salmon, K. (2013). Reasoning about the self in positive and negative ways: Relationship to psychological functioning in young adulthood. *Memory, 21*(1), 10–26.

Banks, M. V. & Salmon, K. (2018). Cognitive response styles and the construction of personal narratives: Implications for psychopathology in young adults. *Imagination, Cognition and Personality, 37*(3), 342–358.

Barry, T. J., Lenaert, B., Hermans, D., Raes, F., & Griffith, J. W. (2018). Meta-analysis of the association between autobiographical memory specificity and exposure to trauma. *Journal of Traumatic Stress, 31*(1), 35–46.

Bech, M., Elklit, A., & Simonsen, E. (2015). Autobiographical memory in borderline personality disorder: A systematic review. *Personality and Mental Health, 9*(2), 162–171.

Beike, D. R., Kleinknecht, E., & Wirth-Beaumont, E. T. (2004). How emotional and nonemotional memories define the self. In D. R. Beike, J. M. Lampinen,

& D. A. Behrend (Eds.), *The self and memory* (pp. 141–159). New York, NY: Psychology Press.

Berna, F., Bennouna-Greene, M., Potheegadoo, J., Verry, P., Conway, M. A., & Danion, J.-M. (2011). Self-defining memories related to illness and their integration into the self in patients with schizophrenia. *Psychiatry Research, 189*(1), 49–54.

Berna, F., Potheegadoo, J., Aouadi, I., Ricarte, J. J., Allé, M. C., et al. (2016). A meta-analysis of autobiographical memory studies in schizophrenia spectrum disorder. *Schizophrenia Bulletin, 42*(1), 56–66.

Berntsen, D. & Rubin, D. C. (2006). The centrality of event scale: A measure of integrating a trauma into one's identity and its relation to post-traumatic stress disorder symptoms. *Behaviour Research and Therapy, 44*(2), 219–231.

Berntsen, D. & Rubin, D. C. (2014). Involuntary memories and dissociative amnesia: Assessing key assumptions in posttraumatic stress disorder research. *Clinical Psychological Science, 2*(2), 174–186.

Berntsen, D., Rubin, D. C., & Siegler, I. C. (2011). Two versions of life: Emotionally negative and positive life events have different roles in the organization of life story and identity. *Emotion, 11*(5), 1190–1201.

Bigler, M., Neimeyer, G. J., & Brown, E. (2001). The divided self revisited: Effects of self-concept clarity and self-concept differentiation on psychological adjustment. *Journal of Social and Clinical Psychology, 20*(3), 396–415.

Blagov, P. S. & Singer, J. A. (2004). Four dimensions of self-defining memories (specificity, meaning, content, and affect) and their relationship to self-restraint, distress, and repressive defensiveness. *Journal of Personality, 72*(3), 481–511.

Bluck, S., Alea, N., Habermas, T., & Rubin, D. C. (2005). A tale of three functions: The self-reported uses of autobiographical memory. *Social Cognition, 23*(1), 91–117.

Bluck, S. & Habermas, T. (2000). The life story schema. *Motivation and Emotion, 24*(2), 121–147.

Boals, A. (2010). Events that have become central to identity: Gender differences in the centrality of events scale for positive and negative events. *Applied Cognitive Psychology, 24*, 107–121.

Brewin, C. R. (2007). Autobiographical memory for trauma: Update on four controversies. *Memory, 15*(3), 227–248.

Brewin, C. R. (2016). Coherence, disorganization, and fragmentation in traumatic memory reconsidered: A response to Rubin et al. (2016). *Journal of Abnormal Psychology, 125*(7), 1011–1017.

Brewin, C. R., Dalgleish, T., & Joseph, S. (1996). A dual representation theory of posttraumatic stress disorder. *Psychological Review, 103*(4), 670–686.

Brewin, C. R., Gregory, J. D., Lipton, M., & Burgess, N. (2010). Intrusive images in psychological disorders: Characteristics, neural mechanisms, and treatment implications. *Psychological Review, 117*(1), 210–232.

Buhlmann, U., Marques, L. M., & Wilhelm, S. (2012). Traumatic experiences in individuals with body dysmorphic disorder. *The Journal of Nervous and Mental Disease, 200*(1), 95–98.

Buhlmann, U., Wilhelm, S., Glaesmer, H., Mewes, R., Brähler, E., & Rief, W. (2011). Perceived appearance-related teasing in body dysmorphic disorder: A population-based survey. *International Journal of Cognitive Therapy, 4*(4), 342–348.

Bullock, G., Newman-Taylor, K., & Stopa, L. (2016). The role of mental imagery in non-clinical paranoia. *Journal of Behavior Therapy and Experimental Psychiatry, 50,* 264–268.

Campbell, J. D., Assanand, S., & Di Paula, A. (2003). The structure of the self-concept and its relation to psychological adjustment. *Journal of Personality, 71*(1), 115–140.

Campbell, J. D., Trapnell, P. D., Heine, S. J., Katz, I. M., Lavallee, L. F., & Lehman, D. R. (1996). Self-concept clarity: Measurement, personality correlates, and cultural boundaries. *Journal of Personality and Social Psychology, 70*(1), 141–156.

Chapman, D. P., Whitfield, C. L., Felitti, V. J., Dube, S. R., Edwards, V. J., & Anda, R. F. (2004). Adverse childhood experiences and the risk of depressive disorders in adulthood. *Journal of Affective Disorders, 82*(2), 217–225.

Çili, S. (2012). *Understanding cognitive changes in imagery rescripting: The role of the memory-imagery-self relationship* (Unpublished doctoral dissertation). University of Southampton, United Kingdom.

Çili, S. & Stopa, L. (2015a). The retrieval of self-defining memories is associated with the activation of specific working selves. *Memory, 23*(2), 233–253.

Çili, S. & Stopa, L. (2015b). Intrusive mental imagery in psychological disorders: Is the self the key to understanding maintenance? *Frontiers in Psychiatry, 6,* 103.

Clark, C., Caldwell, T., Power, C., & Stansfeld, S. A. (2010). Does the influence of childhood adversity on psychopathology persist across the lifecourse? A 45-year prospective epidemiologic study. *Annals of Epidemiology, 20*(5), 385–394.

Clark, D. M. & Wells, A. (1995). A cognitive model of social phobia. In R. G. Heimberg, M. R. Liebowitz, D. A. Hope, & F. R. Schneier (Eds.), *Social phobia: Diagnosis, assessment, and treatment* (pp. 69–93). New York, NY: Guilford Press.

Cockerham, E. S., Çili, S., & Stopa, L. (2016). Investigating the phenomenology of imagery following traumatic burn injuries. *Burns, 42*(4), 853–862.

Conway, M. A., Meares, K., & Standart, S. (2004). Images and goals. *Memory, 12*(4), 525–531.

Conway, M. A., & Pleydell-Pearce, C. W. (2000). The construction of auto-biographical memories in the self-memory system. *Psychological Review, 107*(2), 261–288.

Coughtrey, A. E., Shafran, R., & Rachman, S. J. (2013). Imagery in mental contamination: A questionnaire study. *Journal of Obsessive-Compulsive and Related Disorders, 2*(4), 385–390.

Coughtrey, A. E., Shafran, R., & Rachman, S. J. (2015). Imagery in mental contamination. *Behavioural and Cognitive Psychotherapy, 43*(3), 257–269.

Crane, C., Shah, D., Barnhofer, T., & Holmes, E. A. (2012). Suicidal imagery in a previously depressed community sample. *Clinical Psychology & Psychotherapy, 19*(1), 57–69.

Crespo, M. & Fernández-Lansac, V. (2016). Memory and narrative of traumatic events: A literature review. *Psychological Trauma: Theory, Research, Practice, and Policy*, 8, 149–156.

Dalgleish, T., Hill, E., Golden, A.-M. J., Morant, N., & Dunn, B. D. (2011). The structure of past and future lives in depression. *Journal of Abnormal Psychology, 120*(1), 1–15.

Dalgleish, T., Tchanturia, K., Serpell, L., Hems, S., Yiend, J., et al (2003). Self-reported parental abuse relates to autobiographical memory style in patients with eating disorders. *Emotion, 3*, 211–222.

Dalgleish, T. & Werner-Seidler, A. (2014). Disruptions in autobiographical memory processing in depression and the emergence of memory therapeutics. *Trends in Cognitive Sciences, 18*(11), 596–604.

D'Argembeau, A., Lardi, C., & Van der Linden, M. (2012). Self-defining future projections: Exploring the identity function of thinking about the future. *Memory, 20*(2), 110–120.

Day, S. J., Holmes, E. A., & Hackmann, A. (2004). Occurrence of imagery and its link with early memories in agoraphobia. *Memory, 12*(4), 416–427.

Demblon, J. & D'Argembeau, A. (2017). Contribution of past and future self-defining event networks to personal identity. *Memory, 25*(5), 656–665.

Dempsey, R. C., Gooding, P. A., & Jones, S. H. (2014). Assessing the specificity of autobiographical memory in individuals at a trait-based vulnerability to bipolar disorder using a sentence completion task. *Memory, 22*(3), 222–231.

Di Simplicio, M., Renner, F., Blackwell, S. E., Mitchell, H., Stratford, H. J., et al. (2016). An investigation of mental imagery in bipolar disorder: Exploring "the mind's eye." *Bipolar Disorders, 18*(8), 669–683.

Dugué, R., Keller, S., Tuschen-Caffier, B., & Jacob, G. A. (2016). Exploring the mind's eye: Contents and characteristics of mental images in overweight individuals with binge eating behaviour. *Psychiatry Research, 246*, 554–560.

Ehlers, A. & Clark, D. M. (2000). A cognitive model of posttraumatic stress disorder. *Behaviour Research and Therapy, 38*, 319–345.

Ehlers, A., Hackmann, A., Steil, R., Clohessy, S., Wenninger, K., & Winter, H. (2002). The nature of intrusive memories after trauma: The warning signal hypothesis. *Behaviour Research and Therapy, 40*, 995–1002.

Eich, E., Handy, T. C., Holmes, E. A., Lerner, J., & McIsaac, H. K. (2011, March). *Field and observer perspectives in autobiographical memory*. Chapter presented at the 14th Sydney Symposium on Social Psychology, Sydney, Australia. Retrieved from www.sydneysymposium.unsw.edu.au/2011/chapters/EichSSSP2011.pdf

Eustache, F., Viard, A., & Desgranges, B. (2016). The MNESIS model: Memory systems and processes, identity and future thinking. *Neuropsychologia, 87*, 96–109.

Farrar, S., Stopa, L., & Turner, H. (2015). Self-imagery in individuals with high body dissatisfaction: The effect of positive and negative imagery on aspects of the self-concept. *Journal of Behavior Therapy and Experimental Psychiatry, 46*, 8–13.

Fredrickson, B. L. (2001). The role of positive emotions in positive psychology: The broaden-and-build theory of positive emotions. *American Psychologist, 56*, 218–226.

Goddard, L., Dritschel, B., & Burton, A. (1996). Role of autobiographical memory in social problem solving and depression. *Journal of Abnormal Psychology, 105*(4), 609–616.

Goddard, L., Dritschel, B., & Burton, A. (2001). The effects of specific retrieval instruction on social problem-solving in depression. *British Journal of Clinical Psychology, 40*(3), 297–308.

Graci, M. E., Watts, A. L., & Fivush, R. (2018). Examining the factor structure of narrative meaning-making for stressful events and relations with psychological distress. *Memory*. Advance online publication.

Green, M. (2015). *Aftershock: The untold story of surviving peace.* London, England: Portobello Books.

Greenhoot, A. F., Sun, S., Bunnell, S. L., & Lindboe, K. (2013). Making sense of traumatic memories: Memory qualities and psychological symptoms in emerging adults with and without abuse histories. *Memory, 21*(1), 125–142.

Gregory, J. D., Brewin, C. R., Mansell, W., & Donaldson, C. (2010). Intrusive memories and images in bipolar disorder. *Behaviour Research and Therapy, 48*, 698–703.

Grey, N. (2009). Imagery and psychological threat to the self in PTSD. In L. Stopa (Ed.), *Imagery and the threatened self: Perspectives on mental imagery and the self in cognitive therapy* (pp. 137–165). London, England: Routledge.

Grey, N. & Holmes, E. A. (2008). Hotspots in trauma memories in the treatment of post-traumatic stress disorder: A replication. *Memory, 16*(7), 788–796.

Habermas, T. & Bluck, S. (2000). Getting a life: The emergence of the life story in adolescence. *Psychological Bulletin, 126*(5), 748–769.

Habermas, T. & Köber, C. (2015). Autobiographical reasoning in life narratives buffers the effect of biographical disruptions on the sense of self-continuity. *Memory, 23*(5), 664–674.

Hackmann, A., Clark, D. M., & McManus, F. (2000). Recurrent images and early memories in social phobia. *Behaviour Research and Therapy, 38*(6), 601–610.

Hackmann, A., Day, S., & Holmes, E. A. (2009). Agoraphobia: Imagery and the threatened self. In L. Stopa (Ed.), *Imagery and the threatened self: Perspectives on mental imagery and the self in cognitive therapy* (pp. 112–136). London, England: Routledge.

Hackmann, A., Surawy, C., & Clark, D. M. (1998). Seeing yourself through others' eyes: A study of spontaneously occurring images in social phobia. *Behavioural and Cognitive Psychotherapy, 26*, 3–12.

Hallford, D. J., Austin, D. W., Takano, K., & Raes, F. (2018). Psychopathology and episodic future thinking: A systematic review and meta-analysis of specificity and episodic detail. *Behaviour Research and Therapy, 102*, 42–51.

Hallford, D. J. & Mellor, D. (2017). Autobiographical memory specificity and general symptoms of anxiety: Indirect associations through rumination. *International Journal of Mental Health, 46*(2), 74–88.

Harris, L. S., Block, S. D., Ogle, C. M., Goodman, G. S., Augusti, E.-M., et al. (2016). Coping style and memory specificity in adolescents and adults with histories of child sexual abuse. *Memory, 24*(8), 1078–1090.

Harris, C. B., Rasmussen, A. S., & Berntsen, D. (2014). The functions of autobiographical memory: An integrative approach. *Memory, 22*(5), 559–581.

Hinrichsen, H., Morrison, T., Waller, G., & Schmidt, U. (2007). Triggers of self-induced vomiting in bulimic disorders: The roles of core beliefs and imagery. *Journal of Cognitive Psychotherapy: An International Quarterly, 21*(3), 261–272.

Hitchcock, C., Rees, C., & Dalgleish, T. (2017). The devil's in the detail: Accessibility of specific personal memories supports rose-tinted self-generalizations in mental health and toxic self-generalizations in clinical depression. *Journal of Experimental Psychology: General, 146*(9), 1286–1295.

Holm, T., Pillemer, D. B., Bliksted, V., & Thomsen, D. K. (2017). A decline in self-defining memories following a diagnosis of schizophrenia. *Comprehensive Psychiatry, 76*, 18–25.

Holm, T. & Thomsen, D. K. (2018). Self-event connections in life stories, self-concept clarity, and dissociation: Examining their relations with symptoms of psychopathology. *Imagination, Cognition and Personality, 37*(3), 293–317.

Holm, T., Thomsen, D. K., & Bliksted, V. (2016). Life story chapters and narrative self-continuity in patients with schizophrenia. *Consciousness and Cognition, 45*, 60–74.

Holmes, E. A., Blackwell, S. E., Burnett Heyes, S., Renner, F., & Raes, F. (2016). Mental imagery in depression: Phenomenology, potential mechanisms, and treatment implications. *Annual Review of Clinical Psychology, 12*, 249–280.

Holmes, E. A., Crane, C., Fennell, M. J. V., & Williams, J. M. G. (2007). Imagery about suicide in depression: "Flash-forwards"? *Journal of Behavior Therapy and Experimental Psychiatry, 38*(4), 423–434.

Holmes, E. A., Geddes, J. R., Colom, F., & Goodwin, G. M. (2008). Mental imagery as an emotional amplifier: Application to bipolar disorder. *Behaviour Research and Therapy, 46*, 1251–1258.

Holmes, E. A. & Mathews, A. (2010). Mental imagery in emotion and emotional disorders. *Clinical Psychology Review, 30*(3), 349–362.

Homer, S. R. & Deeprose, C. (2017). Voluntary and involuntary imagery in social anxiety. *Behavioural and Cognitive Psychotherapy, 45*(3), 285–299.

Houle, I. & Philippe, F. L. (2017). Need satisfaction in episodic memories impacts mood at retrieval and well-being over time. *Personality and Individual Differences, 105*, 194–199.

Huntjens, R. J. C., Wessel, I., Hermans, D., & van Minnen, A. (2014). Autobiographical memory specificity in dissociative identity disorder. *Journal of Abnormal Psychology, 123*(2), 419–428.

Huntjens, R. J. C., Wessel, I., Ostafin, B. D., Boelen, P. A., Behrens, F., & van Minnen, A. (2016). Trauma-related self-defining memories and future goals in dissociative identity disorder. *Behaviour Research and Therapy, 87*, 216–224.

Isbell, L. M. & Lair, E. C. (2013). Moods, emotions, and evaluations as information. In D. Carlston (Ed.), *Oxford handbook of social cognition* (pp. 435–462). New York, NY: Oxford University Press.

Isen, A. M. (2004). Some perspectives on positive feelings and emotions: Positive affect facilitates thinking and problem solving. In A. S. R. Manstead, N. Frijda, & A. Fischer (Eds.), *Feelings and emotions: The Amsterdam symposium* (pp. 263–281). Cambridge, England: Cambridge University Press.

Jing, H. G., Madore, K. P., & Schacter, D. L. (2017). Preparing for what might happen: An episodic specificity induction impacts the generation of alternative future events. *Cognition, 169*, 118–128.

Kleim, B. & Ehlers, A. (2008). Reduced autobiographical memory specificity predicts depression and posttraumatic stress disorder after recent trauma. *Journal of Consulting and Clinical Psychology, 76*(2), 231–242.

Kleim, B., Graham, B., Fihosy, S., Stott, R., & Ehlers, A. (2014). Reduced specificity in episodic future thinking in posttraumatic stress disorder. *Clinical Psychological Science, 2*(2), 165–173.

Kosslyn, S. M., Ganis, G., & Thompson, W. L. (2001). Neural foundations of imagery. *Nature, 2*, 635–642.

Kyung, Y., Yanes-Lukin, P., & Roberts, J. E. (2016). Specificity and detail in autobiographical memory: Same or different constructs? *Memory, 24*(2), 272–284.

Lekes, N., Guilbault, V., Philippe, F. L., & Houle, I. (2014). Remembering events related to close relationships, self-growth, and helping others: Intrinsic autobiographical memories, need satisfaction, and well-being. *Journal of Research in Personality, 53*, 103–111.

Liao, H. W., Bluck, S., & Westerhof, G. J. (2018). Longitudinal relations between self-defining memories and self-esteem: Mediating roles of meaning-making and memory function. *Imagination, Cognition and Personality, 37*(3), 318–341.

Libby, L. K., Shaeffer, E. M., Eibach, R. P., & Slemmer, J. A. (2007). Picture yourself at the polls: Visual perspective in mental imagery affects self-perception and behavior. *Psychological Science, 18*(3), 199–203.

Lilgendahl, J. P. & McAdams, D. P. (2011). Constructing stories of self-growth: How individual differences in patterns of autobiographical reasoning relate to well-being in midlife. *Journal of Personality, 79*(2), 391–428.

Lipton, M. G., Brewin, C. R., Linke, S., & Halperin, J. (2010). Distinguishing features of intrusive images in obsessive-compulsive disorder. *Journal of Anxiety Disorders, 24*, 816–822.

Lobbestael, J., Arntz, A., & Bernstein, D. P. (2010). Disentangling the relationship between different types of childhood maltreatment and personality disorders. *Journal of Personality Disorders, 24*(3), 285–295.

Lodi-Smith, J., Geise, A. C., Roberts, B. W., & Robins, R. W. (2009). Narrating personality change. *Journal of Personality and Social Psychology, 96*(3), 679–689.

Luchetti, M., Rossi, N., Montebarocci, O., & Sutin, A. R. (2016). Continuity of phenomenology and (in)consistency of content of meaningful autobiographical memories. *Consciousness and Cognition, 42*, 15–25.

Mansell, W. & Hodson, S. (2009). Imagery and memories of the social self in people with bipolar disorders: Empirical evidence, phenomenology, theory and therapy. In L. Stopa (Ed.), *Imagery and the threatened self: Perspectives on mental imagery and the self in cognitive therapy* (pp. 232–264). London, England: Routledge.

Mansell, W. & Lam, D. (2004). A preliminary study of autobiographical memory in remitted bipolar and unipolar depression and the role of imagery in the specificity of memory. *Memory, 12*(4), 437–446.

Maurex, L., Lekander, M., Nilsonne, Å., Andersson, E. E., Åsberg, M., & Öhman, A. (2010). Social problem solving, autobiographical memory, trauma, and depression in women with borderline personality disorder and a history of suicide attempts. *British Journal of Clinical Psychology, 49*(3), 327–342.

McAdams, D. P. (2015). *The art and science of personality development.* New York, NY: Guilford Press.

McAdams, D. P., Reynolds, J., Lewis, M., Patten, A. H., & Bowman, P. J. (2001). When bad things turn good and good things turn bad: Sequences of redemption and contamination in life narrative and their relation to psychosocial adaptation in midlife adults and in students. *Personality and Social Psychology Bulletin, 27*(4), 474–485.

McCoy, T. P. & Dunlop, W. L. (2017). Down on the upside: Redemption, contamination, and agency in the lives of adult children of alcoholics. *Memory, 25*(5), 586–594.

McKay, C., Castagna, P., Singer, J. A., & Conway, M. A. (in press). Psychological disorders and autobiographical memories: Examining memory specificity, affective content, and meaning-making. In A. Mishara, P. Corlett, P. Fletcher, & M. Schwartz (Eds.), *Phenomenological neuropsychiatry: How patient experience bridges clinic with clinical neuroscience.* New York, NY: Springer.

McLean, K. C. & Breen, A. V. (2009). Processes and content of narrative identity development in adolescence: Gender and well-being. *Developmental Psychology, 45*(3), 702–710.

McLean, K. C., Breen, A. V., & Fournier, M. A. (2010). Constructing the self in early, middle, and late adolescent boys: Narrative identity, individuation, and well-being. *Journal of Research on Adolescence, 20*(1), 166–187.

McLean, K. C. & Pratt, M. W. (2006). Life's little (and big) lessons: Identity statuses and meaning-making in the turning point narratives of emerging adults. *Developmental Psychology, 42*(4), 714–722.

McLean, K. C. & Thorne, A. (2003). Late adolescents' self-defining memories about relationships. *Developmental Psychology, 39*, 635–645.

Merrill, N., Waters, T. E. A., & Fivush, R. (2016). Connecting the self to traumatic and positive events: Links to identity and well-being. *Memory, 24*(10), 1321–1328.

Mihailova, S. & Jobson, L. (2018). Association between intrusive negative autobiographical memories and depression: A meta-analytic investigation. *Clinical Psychology and Psychotherapy.* Advance online publication.

Moffitt, K. H. & Singer, J. A. (1994). Continuity in the life story: Self-defining memories, affect, and approach/avoidance personal strivings. *Journal of Personality, 62*(1), 21–43.

Moore, S. A. & Zoellner, L. A. (2007). Overgeneral autobiographical memory and traumatic events: An evaluative review. *Psychological Bulletin, 133*(3), 419–437.

Morina, N., Deeprose, C., Pusowski, C., Schmid, M., & Holmes, E. A. (2011). Prospective mental imagery in patients with major depressive disorder or anxiety disorders. *Journal of Anxiety Disorders, 25*(8), 1032–1037.

Morrison, A. P., Beck, A. T., Glentworth, D., Dunn, H., Reid, G. S., et al. (2002). Imagery and psychotic symptoms: A preliminary investigation. *Behaviour Research and Therapy, 40*(9), 1053–1062.

Muse, K., McManus, F., Hackmann, A., Williams, M., & Williams, M. (2010). Intrusive imagery in severe health anxiety: Prevalence, nature and links with memories and maintenance cycles. *Behaviour Research and Therapy, 48,* 792–798.

Mutlutürk, A. & Tekcan, A. İ. (2016). Remembering and telling self-consistent and self-discrepant memories. *Memory, 24*(4), 513–525.

Nandrino, J.-L. & Gandolphe, M.-C. (2017). Characterization of self-defining memories in individuals with severe alcohol use disorders after mid-term abstinence: The impact of the emotional valence of memories. *Alcoholism: Clinical and Experimental Research, 41*(8), 1484–1491.

Nandrino, J.-L., Gandolphe, M.-C., & El Haj, M. (2017). Autobiographical memory compromise in individuals with alcohol use disorders: Towards implications for psychotherapy research. *Drug and Alcohol Dependence, 179,* 61–70.

Ng, A. S., Abbott, M. J., & Hunt, C. (2014). The effect of self-imagery on symptoms and processes in social anxiety: A systematic review. *Clinical Psychology Review, 34*(8), 620–633.

Ng, R. M. K., Di Simplicio, M., McManus, F., Kennerley, H., & Holmes, E. A. (2016). 'Flash-forwards' and suicidal ideation: A prospective investigation of mental imagery, entrapment and defeat in a cohort from the Hong Kong Mental Morbidity Survey. *Psychiatry Research, 246,* 453–460.

Norton, A. R. & Abbott, M. J. (2017). Bridging the gap between aetiological and maintaining factors in social anxiety disorder: The impact of socially traumatic experiences on beliefs, imagery and symptomatology. *Clinical Psychology and Psychotherapy, 24*(3), 747–765.

O'Donnell, C., Di Simplicio, M., Brown, R., Holmes, E. A., & Burnett Heyes, S. (2017). The role of mental imagery in mood amplification: An investigation across subclinical features of bipolar disorders. *Cortex.* Advance online publication.

Osman, S., Cooper, M., Hackmann, A., & Veale, D. (2004). Spontaneously occurring images and early memories in people with body dysmorphic disorder. *Memory, 12*(4), 428–436.

Pals, J. L. (2006). Narrative identity processing of difficult life experiences: Pathways of personality development and positive self-transformation in adulthood. *Journal of Personality, 74*(4), 1079–1110.

Paradise, A. W. & Kernis, M. H. (2002). Self-esteem and psychological well-being: Implications of fragile self-esteem. *Journal of Social and Clinical Psychology, 21*, 345–361.

Park, C. L. (2010). Making sense of the meaning literature: An integrative review of meaning making and its effects on adjustment to stressful life events. *Psychological Bulletin, 136*(2), 257–301.

Patel, T., Brewin, C. R., Wheatley, J., Wells, A., Fisher, P., & Myers, S. (2007). Intrusive images and memories in major depression. *Behaviour Research and Therapy, 45*(11), 2573–2580.

Pearson, J., Naselaris, T., Holmes, E. A., & Kosslyn, S. M. (2015). Mental imagery: Functional mechanisms and clinical applications. *Trends in Cognitive Sciences, 19*(10), 590–602.

Pedersen, A. M., Straarup, K. N., & Thomsen, D. K. (2018). Narrative identity in female patients with remitted bipolar disorder: A negative past and a foreshortened future. *Memory, 26*(2), 219–228.

Philippe, F. L. & Bernard-Desrosiers, L. (2017). The odyssey of episodic memories: Identifying the paths and processes through which they contribute to well-being. *Journal of Personality, 85*(4), 518–529.

Philippe, F. L., Koestner, R., Beaulieu-Pelletier, G., & Lecours, S. (2011). The role of need satisfaction as a distinct and basic psychological component of autobiographical memories: A look at well-being. *Journal of Personality, 79*(5), 905–938.

Price, K., Veale, D., & Brewin, C. R. (2012). Intrusive imagery in people with a specific phobia of vomiting. *Journal of Behavior Therapy and Experimental Psychiatry, 43*(1), 672–678.

Raes, F., Hermans, D., Williams, J. M. G., Beyers, W., Brunfaut, E., & Eelen, P. (2006). Reduced autobiographical memory specificity and rumination in predicting the course of depression. *Journal of Abnormal Psychology, 115*(4), 699–704.

Raffard, S., Bortolon, C., D'Argembeau, A., Gardes, J., Gely-Nargeot, M.-C., et al. (2016). Projecting the self into the future in individuals with schizophrenia: A preliminary cross-sectional study. *Memory, 24*(6), 826–837.

Raffard, S., D'Argembeau, A., Lardi, C., Bayard, S., Boulenger, J.-P., & Van Der Linden, M. (2009). Exploring self-defining memories in schizophrenia. *Memory, 17*(1), 26–38.

Raffard, S., D'Argembeau, A., Lardi, C., Bayard, S., Boulenger, J.-P., & Van der Linden, M. (2010). Narrative identity in schizophrenia. *Consciousness and Cognition, 19*(1), 328–340.

Raffard, S., Esposito, F., Boulenger, J. P., & Van der Linden, M. (2013). Impaired ability to imagine future pleasant events is associated with apathy in schizophrenia. *Psychiatry Research, 209*(3), 393–400.

Rasmussen, A. S. & Berntsen, D. (2011). The unpredictable past: Spontaneous autobiographical memories outnumber autobiographical memories retrieved strategically. *Consciousness and Cognition, 20*(4), 1842–1846.

Rasmussen, A. S., Jørgensen, C. R., O'Connor, M., Bennedsen, B. E., Godt, K. D., et al. (2017). The structure of past and future events in borderline personality disorder, eating disorder, and obsessive-compulsive disorder. *Psychology of Consciousness: Theory, Research, and Practice, 4*(2), 190–210.

Reese, E., Myftari, E., McAnally, H. M., Chen, Y., Neha, T., et al. (2017). Telling the tale and living well: Adolescent narrative identity, personality traits, and well-being across cultures. *Child Development, 88*(2), 612–628.

Remmers, C. & Zander, T. (2018). Why you don't see the forest for the trees when you are anxious: Anxiety impairs intuitive decision making. *Clinical Psychological Science, 6*(1), 48–62.

Reynolds, M. & Brewin, C. R. (1999). Intrusive memories in depression and posttraumatic stress disorder. *Behaviour Research and Therapy, 37*, 201–215.

Ricarte, J. J., Ros, L., Latorre, J. M., & Watkins, E. (2017). Mapping auto-biographical memory in schizophrenia: Clinical implications. *Clinical Psychology Review, 51*, 96–108.

Rubin, D. C., Berntsen, D., Ogle, C. M., Deffler, S. A., & Beckham, J. C. (2016). Scientific evidence versus outdated beliefs: A response to Brewin (2016). *Journal of Abnormal Psychology, 125*, 1018–1021.

Sales, J. M., Merrill, N. A., & Fivush, R. (2013). Does making meaning make it better? Narrative meaning making and well-being in at-risk African-American adolescent females. *Memory, 21*(1), 97–110.

Schacter, D. L., Addis, D. R., Hassabis, D., Martin, V. C., Spreng, R. N., & Szpunar, K. K. (2012). The future of memory: Remembering, imagining, and the brain. *Neuron, 76*(4), 677–694.

Schulze, K., Freeman, D., Green, C., & Kuipers, E. (2013). Intrusive mental imagery in patients with persecutory delusions. *Behaviour Research and Therapy, 51*(1), 7–14.

Scott, J., Stanton, B., Garland, A., & Ferrier, I. N. (2000). Cognitive vulnerability in patients with bipolar disorder. *Psychological Medicine, 30*(2), 467–472.

Sedikides, C., Green, J. D., & Pinter, B. (2004). Self-protective memory. In D. R., Beike, J. M. Lampinen, & D. A. Behrend (Eds.), *The self and memory* (pp. 161–179). New York, NY: Psychology Press.

Singer, J. A. (1997). *Message in a bottle: Stories of men and addiction.* New York, NY: Free Press.

Singer, J. A. & Blagov, P. S. (2000). *Classification system and scoring manual for self-defining autobiographical memories.* Unpublished manuscript, Department of Psychology, Connecticut College, New London, CT.

Singer, J. A., Blagov, P., Berry, M., & Oost, K. M. (2013). Self-defining mem-ories, scripts, and the life story: Narrative identity in personality and psycho-therapy. *Journal of Personality, 81*(6), 569–582.

Somerville, K., Cooper, M., & Hackmann, A. (2007). Spontaneous imagery in women with bulimia nervosa: An investigation into content, characteristics and links to childhood memories. *Journal of Behavior Therapy and Experimental Psychiatry, 38*(4), 435–446.

Speckens, A. E. M., Hackmann, A., Ehlers, A., & Cuthbert, B. (2007). Imagery special issue: Intrusive images and memories of earlier adverse events in patients with obsessive compulsive disorder. *Journal of Behavior Therapy and Experimental Psychiatry, 38*(4), 411–422.

Spinhoven, P., Bamelis, L., Molendijk, M., Haringsma, R., & Arntz, A. (2009). Reduced specificity of autobiographical memory in Cluster C personality disorders and the role of depression, worry, and experiential avoidance. *Journal of Abnormal Psychology, 118*(3), 520–530.

Steiner, K. L., Thomsen, D. K., & Pillemer, D. B. (2017). Life story chapters, specific memories, and conceptions of the self. *Applied Cognitive Psychology, 31*(5), 478–487.

Stopa, L. (2009). Reconceptualizing the self. *Cognitive and Behavioral Practice, 16*(2), 142–148.

Stopa, L., Brown, M. A., Luke, M. A., & Hirsch, C. R. (2010). Constructing a self: The role of self-structure and self-certainty in social anxiety. *Behaviour Research and Therapy, 48*(10), 955–965.

Sutherland, K. & Bryant, R. A. (2005). Self-defining memories in post-traumatic stress disorder. *British Journal of Clinical Psychology, 44*(4), 591–598.

Szpunar, K. K. (2010). Episodic future thought: An emerging concept. *Perspectives on Psychological Science, 5*(2), 142–162.

Thomsen, D. K., Lind, M., & Pillemer, D. B. (2017). Examining relations between aging, life story chapters, and well-being. *Applied Cognitive Psychology, 31*(2), 207–215.

Thomsen, D. K., Olesen, M. H., Schnieber, A., & Tønnesvang, J. (2014). The emotional content of life stories: Positivity bias and relation to personality. *Cognition and Emotion, 28*(2), 260–277.

Tzemou, E. & Birchwood, M. (2007). A prospective study of dysfunctional thinking and the regulation of negative intrusive memories in bipolar 1 disorder: Implications for affect regulation theory. *Psychological Medicine, 37*, 689–698.

Van den Broeck, K., Claes, L., Pieters, G., Hermans, D., & Raes, F. (2015). Overgeneral memory in borderline personality disorder. In L. A. Watson & D. Berntsen (Eds.), *Clinical perspectives on autobiographical memory* (pp. 221–241). Cambridge, England: Cambridge University Press.

Wade, D. M., Brewin, C. R., Howell, D. C. J., White, E., Mythen, M. G., & Weinman, J. A. (2015). Intrusive memories of hallucinations and delusions in traumatized intensive care patients: An interview study. *British Journal of Health Psychology, 20*(3), 613–631.

Walentynowicz, M., Raes, F., Van Diest, I., & Van den Bergh, O. (2017). The specificity of health-related autobiographical memories in patients with somatic symptom disorder. *Psychosomatic Medicine, 79*(1), 43–49.

Waters, T. E. A., Shallcross, J. F., & Fivush, R. (2013). The many facets of meaning making: Comparing multiple measures of meaning making and their relations to psychological distress. *Memory, 21*(1), 111–124.

Wells, A., Clark. D. M., & Ahmad, S. (1998). How do I look with my mind's eye: Perspective taking in social phobic imagery. *Behaviour Research and Therapy, 36*(6), 631–634.

Wells, A. & Hackmann, A. (1993). Imagery and core beliefs in health anxiety: Content and origins. *Behavioural and Cognitive Psychotherapy, 21*, 265–273.

Werner-Seidler, A. & Moulds, M. L. (2011). Autobiographical memory characteristics in depression vulnerability: Formerly depressed individuals recall less vivid positive memories. *Cognition and Emotion, 25*(6), 1087–1103.

Weßlau, C., Lieberz, K., Oertel-Knöchel, V., & Steil, R. (2016). Distressing visual mental images in depressed patients and healthy controls: Are they one and the same? *Psychiatry Research, 246,* 341–347.

Weststrate, N. M. & Glück, J. (2017). Hard-earned wisdom: Exploratory processing of difficult life experience is positively associated with wisdom. *Developmental Psychology, 53*(4), 800–814.

Williams, J. M. G., Barnhofer, T., Crane, C., Hermans, D., Raes, F., et al. (2007). Autobiographical memory specificity and emotional disorder. *Psychological Bulletin, 133*(1), 122–148.

Wilson, A. E. & Ross, M. (2003). The identity function of autobiographical memory: Time is on our side. *Memory, 11*(2), 137–149.

Zaragoza Scherman, A., Salgado, S., Shao, Z., & Berntsen, D. (2015). Event centrality of positive and negative autobiographical memories to identity and life story across cultures. *Memory, 23*(8), 1152–1171.

5 Implications of the memory-self relationship and narrative identity literature for cognitive-behavioural therapy

Introduction

As discussed in the previous chapter, autobiographical memories (AMs) play an important role in psychopathology. Their content, affective tone, specificity, as well as their narrative structure and meaning, can influence the way in which AMs execute their self and directive functions. Among other things, AMs and associated mental images can contribute to the development of a negative sense of self, disruptions in self-continuity, chronic negative affect, and maladaptive behaviours. Because of their importance for personality development and psychopathology, AMs – whether repressed or remembered – have played an important role in psychotherapy since the 19th century (see Edwards, 2007; Singer & Salovey, 1993). They have been used not only to understand patients' symptoms, but also to address them.

Among the therapies that rely on and target patients' adverse AMs is cognitive-behavioural therapy (CBT). This family of therapies incorporates the memory-imagery-self relationship in its conceptualisation of psychopathology and focuses on modifying maladaptive thoughts, images, and beliefs that derive from individuals' interpretation of their experiences. In the last few decades, CBT has seen a surge in the number of therapeutic techniques that aim to modify the affective tone of and meanings associated with distressing memories or intrusive images, as well as techniques that train individuals to retrieve particular AMs (e.g., specific rather than overgeneral ones) (see Dalgleish & Werner-Seidler, 2014; Hitchcock, Werner-Seidler, Blackwell, & Dalgleish, 2017; Holmes, Arntz, & Smucker, 2007). The aim of this chapter is to discuss some of the techniques used in CBT to address distressing memories and associated images and reflect on the implications of the memory-self relationship for these techniques and for CBT in general. The chapter begins with an overview of the generic cognitive model, which underpins CBT. We then focus on how negative meanings and the self are incorporated in different cognitive-behavioural interventions and discuss the potential mechanisms through which these interventions might promote therapeutic change. We conclude with a reflection on how the narrative identity literature can be used to enhance our understanding of CBT and to inform CBT practice.

The generic cognitive model

The origins of the current family of cognitive-behavioural therapies date back to Aaron T. Beck's model of depression (Beck, Rush, Shaw, & Emery, 1979) and its development in the field of anxiety (Beck, Emery, & Greenberg, 1985). The core of the generic cognitive model is the idea that individuals possess cognitive schemas containing memories; goals; expectations; and core beliefs about the self, others, and the world (Beck & Dozois, 2011; Beck et al., 1979; Padesky, 1994). These schemas influence how they organise and process information and guide their affective, behavioural, and physiological responses to situational stimuli (Beck & Dozois, 2011; Beck et al., 1979; J. S. Beck, 2011; Padesky, 1994). According to the original model, schemas develop as a result of unique or repeated life experiences (Beck, 1967; Beck et al., 1979) and "become increasingly consolidated and organized as new experiences are assimilated into the existing belief structure" (Beck & Dozois, 2011, p. 399). The beliefs they contain are based on individuals' interpretations of their experiences. When these beliefs and meanings are negative (e.g., *"I am unlovable," "Others cannot be trusted," "The world is dangerous"*), they contribute to psychological distress. In fact, negative beliefs and self-views related to adverse experiences are at the centre of a number of current cognitive models of disorders, including social anxiety (Clark & Wells, 1995), posttraumatic stress disorder (PTSD; Ehlers & Clark, 2000), eating disorders (e.g., Cooper, Wells, & Todd, 2004), and borderline personality disorder (BPD; Young, 1999).

CBT and its focus on adverse memories and mental images

In traditional CBT, cognitive conceptualisations of patients' issues can have either a longitudinal or a cross-sectional focus. Longitudinal conceptualisations include identification of dysfunctional beliefs and/or behaviours, their potential origins, and their contribution to symptom development and maintenance. Cross-sectional formulations, which are at the heart of many current disorder-specific models, acknowledge the potential influence of AMs in the development of negative beliefs and views of self, but focus on understanding the processes maintaining current symptom patterns. At the centre of Clark and Wells' (1995) model of social anxiety disorder, for example, is the idea that negative and dysfunctional views of self are represented by a negative image or "felt sense" that often relates to earlier memories. These images are interpreted as realistic views of how the person appears to others and drive perceptions of danger and anxiety in social situations, in addition to physiological, cognitive, and behavioural responses (e.g., speaking quickly to avoid pauses). In these situations, patients become preoccupied with how they are appearing to others and focus their attention on themselves instead of focusing on what is happening around them. In the long run, self-focused attention and maladaptive responses to threatening social situations prevent them from obtaining information that can challenge their dysfunctional self-views and help maintain symptoms.

In the disorder-specific models of anxiety now available, treatment focuses initially on targeting the hypothesised maintaining processes and alleviating symptoms rather than on examining the potential role of earlier experiences and AMs. Treatment for generalised anxiety disorder, for example, concentrates on the management of negative affect, worry, and behaviours, as well as on teaching patients to make less threatening and more benign interpretations of internal and external stimuli or the future (see Hirsch & Mathews, 2012). In this and other disorders, treatment can also include behavioural experiments, which are often designed to test out the veracity of patients' beliefs rather than explore the origins of these beliefs. For example, current treatments for social anxiety use experiments to challenge distorted negative images of the self in social situations (e.g., filming patients while talking to a stranger and then having them watch the video) and to test catastrophic predictions (e.g., having patients drop something at a shop and then check how people actually react) (see Clark, 2001; Fang, Sawyer, Asnaani, & Hofmann, 2013). Beliefs can also be challenged using techniques such as cognitive reappraisal, continua, and positive data logs that record information and experiences that are contrary to the maladaptive belief and consonant with a new belief that the patient has formulated through evidence reviews. Key to these interventions is the fact that therapists need to know patients' beliefs, as well as the processes (e.g., selective attention, rumination) and behaviours (e.g., avoidance, withdrawal) that are initiated by the activation of these beliefs.

AMs that have contributed to the development of patients' core beliefs can become a target later in therapy. Therapists can explore the origins of these beliefs through questions such as *"When was the first time that you thought you are unlovable?"* (see Beck, 2011). They can also use questions such as *"What does this experience say about you as a person / other people / the world or life in general?"* in order to obtain a better understanding of the beliefs. When therapists do focus on distressing memories, they can work verbally using techniques such as Socratic questioning and thought challenging and/or with imagery techniques such as exposure and imagery rescripting (ImRs). Although verbal evaluations of distressing memories and their associated meanings can be effective, they are based primarily on logic and often lead to cognitive rather than emotional shifts in beliefs. As a result, some patients report that they *know* that the belief is inaccurate or distorted, but that they do not *feel* or *believe* this on an emotional level (see Arntz & Weertman, 1999). In recent years, cognitive-behavioural therapists have thus increasingly incorporated experiential techniques to effect necessary emotional changes (see Arntz & Weertman, 1999; Thoma & McKay, 2015). These techniques are based on the argument that negative beliefs or self-views often originate from emotional life experiences, so modifying them requires working with the associated AMs and emotions. They often involve exploring relevant negative memories and/or images and then intervening either through an exposure-based technique or through an intervention such as ImRs that aims to change the meanings associated with particular AMs (see Stopa, 2009). Although there are other experiential techniques, for example the empty chair and the two-chair methods pioneered in Gestalt therapy (see Elliott, Watson, Goldman, & Greenberg, 2004), as well as other types of imagery interventions (e.g., image substitution, compassionate imagery) (see Holmes et al., 2007), in this chapter we are focusing primarily on imagery exposure techniques and ImRs because of their direct roles in targeting AMs, images, and associated meanings.

One of the first successes in using imaginal exposure to alleviate distressing memories came with the development of *prolonged exposure (PE)* to treat trauma memories (e.g., Foa, Rothbaum, Riggs, & Murdock, 1991). The aim of PE is to put the trauma memory in context, reduce the associated anxiety and avoidance of the memory and its reminders, and allow patients to obtain corrective information that challenges the distorted beliefs associated with the trauma (McLean & Foa, 2011). It involves repeated exposure to traumatic or disruptive memories during which patients imagine and describe the events in the present tense as the therapist prompts them to recall what happened, who was present during the event, what they perceived (e.g., saw, smelled, heard) at the time, what thoughts went through their mind, and what emotions they experienced. At the end of each session, the therapist and patient engage in post-exposure processing, which involves discussing the patients' experience of the exposure and reflecting on the lessons learnt from it. Exposure is usually repeated within a session or across multiple sessions until the distress associated with the trauma memory is reduced significantly. The underlying assumption of PE is that exposure activates the fear network and that new information gained throughout the process (e.g., the knowledge that one is now safe) alters this network, leading to a reduction in distress (Foa & Kozak, 1986).

More recent models of PTSD (e.g., Ehlers & Clark, 2000) refer to *imaginal reliving (IR)* rather than PE and conceptualise the task as one of memory integration and challenges to the negative meanings associated with the trauma and its sequelae. IR usually involves reliving the trauma as a whole at the outset (similar to PE), but can then move on to identifying and reliving hotspots (moments of peak emotion) that are associated with particular meanings (see Ehlers & Clark, 2008; Ehlers, Clark, Hackmann, McManus, & Fennell, 2005). Unlike PE, IR is not based on a habituation model of change but instead focuses on the need to modify beliefs. This may involve incorporating into the memory information acquired after the trauma (e.g., *"I thought I was going to die when the car was about to crash, but now I know that didn't happen"*). It can also build in knowledge about what was and was not possible at the time the trauma was happening (e.g., *"I thought the accident was my fault, but there is no way I could have stopped it because everything happened so quickly"*). There are a variety of techniques that are used with IR to help embed new learning, for example activating the new belief *("I had to make a snap decision")* during reliving, imagining the post-trauma outcome (e.g., seeing oneself alive and happy with the children), or performing actions that are incompatible with the original meaning (e.g., jumping to prove that one is alive if the original meaning referred to death) (Ehlers & Clark, 2008; Ehlers et al., 2005).

In many cases, IR can spontaneously lead to the discovery of new information and the creation of alternative interpretations and meanings. However, this does not always happen and *ImRs* can be added to the intervention. ImRs describes a group of techniques which originate from Pierre Janet's work and whose explicit aim is to modify distressing memories or images and their meanings (see Edwards, 2007). Although it can be used to change intrusive images that are the product of patients' imagination, it is primarily used to target memory-related images (see Holmes et al., 2007). One of the most commonly used modern ImRs protocols was originally developed by Smucker, Dancu, Foa, and Niederee (1995) to treat victims of childhood sexual abuse suffering from PTSD. It was subsequently adapted by Arntz and

Weertman (1999) to target maladaptive beliefs and complex issues in patients with personality disorders. The protocol developed by Arntz and Weertman includes three stages. In the first stage, patients relive the negative experience. In the second stage, they relive their experience again but from the perspective of their current self. They are asked if they would like to intervene in the memory, for example by entering the scene as adults in order to help the younger self (i.e., the self in the scene being rescripted) or by bringing in other people. The aim is to help patients modify beliefs related to helplessness, vulnerability, or powerlessness and challenge beliefs about the self as bad, unlovable, or somehow responsible for what happened (Smucker & Niederee, 1995). In the third stage, patients visualise the scene and the interaction between their current and younger selves from the younger self's perspective. They are asked to express the younger self's reactions to the adult's intervention and to indicate what, if anything, they want from the adult in order to feel satisfied. The aim is to allow the new meanings to be integrated into patients' schemas from the same perspective as the original event and to teach patients to acknowledge and express needs that they may have learnt to suppress in the past (Arntz & Weertman, 1999). At the end of the session, the therapist and patient discuss what happened during rescripting. The number of sessions required to work on a memory depends on the nature of the memory and patients' problems. For complex issues such as multiple traumas or childhood physical or sexual abuse, different memories may be targeted in different sessions.

Effectiveness of CBT and memory-focused interventions

Overall, CBT is highly effective in treating a range of disorders (Butler, Chapman, Forman, & Beck, 2006; Hofmann, Asnaani, Vonk, Sawyer, & Fang, 2012). The experiential techniques highlighted earlier provide important additional tools with growing evidence for their effectiveness. For example, imaginal exposure combined with cognitive restructuring can alleviate PTSD symptoms in some patients and reduced PTSD symptoms are associated with reduced overgeneral retrieval for positive memories (Sutherland & Bryant, 2007). CBT incorporating IR for intrusive memories in PTSD patients can reduce the intrusions' frequency and distress, as well as the sense of reliving associated with them (Hackmann, Ehlers, Speckens, & Clark, 2004). PE is effective in addressing PTSD symptoms and comorbid issues (e.g., anxiety and depression) in trauma survivors (see McLean & Foa, 2011; Powers, Halpern, Ferenschak, Gillihan, & Foa, 2010). It may be as effective as

ImRs in reducing PTSD symptoms and emotions such as guilt or shame (Langkaas et al., 2017). In fact, imaginal exposure combined with ImRs may be as effective as exposure used on its own in treating PTSD symptoms (Arntz, Tiesema, & Kindt, 2007). In some cases, however, PE may cause an exacerbation of symptoms because of the powerful emotional impact it can have on patients (see Grunert, Smucker, Weis, & Rusch, 2003).

Unlike PE and IR, which have been used primarily with trauma memories in PTSD, ImRs has been used with both traumatic and less severe negative experiences in a variety of disorders characterised by intrusive images. In a recent meta-analysis involving 19 studies that used ImRs to rescript adverse memories, Morina, Lancee, and Arntz (2017) found that this technique is highly effective. Indeed, it alleviated symptoms in social anxiety disorder (Frets, Kevenaar, & van der Heiden, 2014; Lee & Kwon, 2013; Nilsson, Lundh, & Viborg, 2012; Reimer & Moscovitch, 2015; Wild, Hackmann, & Clark, 2007, 2008), PTSD (Arntz, Sofi, & Van Breukelen, 2013; Grunert et al., 2003; Raabe, Ehring, Marquenie, Olff, & Kindt, 2015), depression (Brewin et al., 2009), body dysmorphic disorder (Ritter & Stangier, 2016; Willson, Veale, & Freeston, 2016), and obsessive-compulsive disorder (Veale, Page, Woodward, & Salkovskis, 2015). Some evidence suggests that ImRs may also be beneficial in personality disorders (Weertman & Arntz, 2007) and psychosis (Ison, Medoro, Keen, & Kuipers, 2014).

Because of the extensive evidence on its effectiveness and the evidence base investigating its theoretical underpinnings and mechanisms of change, CBT is seen by some scholars as the gold standard in psychotherapy (see David, Cristea, & Hofmann, 2018). However, there is still plenty of room for improvement. It is not equally effective for all disorders, and for some disorders (e.g., schizophrenia) it may not be superior to other treatments (see Hofmann et al., 2012). Furthermore, not all patients respond to CBT and a significant proportion of people relapse (e.g., Lynch, Laws, & McKenna, 2010). Given the importance of the links between AM and the self described in previous chapters and their potential role in maintaining distress, we believe that a better understanding of the mechanisms underlying change offers the potential for enhancing current treatments.

Mechanisms of change in memory-focused cognitive-behavioural interventions

CBT has been traditionally assumed to work primarily by modifying maladaptive beliefs and schemas (e.g., Padesky, 1994). In this formulation, therapy helps patients to realise that their negative beliefs are distorted and facilitates the incorporation of new, positive information about themselves in their existing schemas. In contrast, Brewin (2006) argues that CBT modifies the *accessibility* of schemas or self-representations rather than changing their content. His retrieval competition hypothesis is based on the argument that individuals possess multiple schemas or self-representations which compete for retrieval in the presence of internal or external cues. Which representations become activated in response to cues depends on factors such as their valence, salience, or the extent to which individuals have rehearsed them. For patients suffering from psychological disorders, negative representations may be salient and well-rehearsed, so they are more likely to be activated compared to positive representations. According to Brewin, CBT helps patients create and/or strengthen positive representations, which then compete for retrieval with their habitual negative representations. Deliberate, repeated activation strengthens the ability of these positive representations to "win" the retrieval competition and inhibit the problematic negative representations (Brewin, 2006).

The debate on exactly how CBT works is ongoing and may be difficult to settle. Whether it works by modifying schema content or by altering accessibility, however, there is a general agreement that CBT does involve changes in meanings (e.g., reinterpretation of experiences) and in self-views. The latter is illustrated in a systematic review on CBT for social anxiety disorder in which Gregory and Peters (2017) conclude that changes in self content and in the processing of self-related information are crucial to CBT. These authors found that, overall, the literature reveals significant reductions in negative, and significant increases in positive, self-related thoughts and beliefs following CBT. These changes often predict and/or mediate treatment outcomes. In fact, Gregory, Wong, Marker, and Peters (2018) found that changes in maladaptive self-beliefs during CBT for social anxiety disorder predict later changes in symptom severity.

The importance of meaning and the self in CBT is also illustrated by evidence on the mechanisms of change in interventions such as PE and ImRs. When it comes to PE, there is an ongoing debate with regards to mechanisms of change (for a review, see Cooper, Clifton, & Feeny, 2017). As noted earlier, several explanations are based on the emotional processing theory, which argues that distressing memories need to be activated before it is possible to modify them (Foa & Kozak, 1986). The idea is that exposure helps patients to process the memories on an emotional level and develop new insights or attach new meanings to them (Cooper et al., 2017; Foa & Kozak, 1986). Other mechanisms may also be involved, such as habituation and subsequent diminished responding (e.g., in terms of distress) to the memory and its reminders, together with enhanced organisation of the trauma narrative (e.g., in terms of temporal ordering or detail) (Cooper et al., 2017). As Cooper and colleagues (2017) point out, however, the evidence on these proposed mechanisms is inconsistent and the change in trauma-related beliefs is one of the few mechanisms that have been consistently supported.

In the case of ImRs, multiple mechanisms of change have been proposed. Arntz (e.g., Arntz, 2011; Arntz & Weertman, 1999; Dibbets & Arntz, 2016) argues that ImRs might work by modifying the meaning of the adverse memory representation (i.e., re-evaluating the unconditioned stimulus representation), which then leads to conditioned stimuli (e.g., trauma reminders) eliciting different or diminished conditioned responses (e.g., emotions) that reflect the new meanings. Brewin, Gregory, Lipton, and Burgess (2010) argue that ImRs may add contextual information to the predominantly sensory representations of the adverse memory (see Chapter 4), thus creating more elaborated representations that effectively compete for retrieval against the old representations. Other explanations include ImRs facilitating the integration of the memory within patients' autobiographical knowledge and allowing the expression of responses (e.g., emotions) that were not expressed during the adverse experience (see Dibbets & Arntz, 2016). Understanding exactly which mechanisms of change are involved in ImRs is difficult because sample sizes in ImRs studies are generally small, randomised controlled trials are scarce, and follow-up periods are often short (see Morina et al., 2017). Nevertheless, it is clear from the existing evidence that ImRs often reduces the strength of the encapsulated belief associated with intrusive images, as well as the distress associated with the targeted memories and images (e.g., Lee & Kwon, 2013; Nilsson et al., 2012; Øktedalen, Hoffart, & Langkaas, 2015; Ritter & Stangier, 2016; Wild et al., 2007, 2008). Reimer and Moscovitch (2015) found that participants with social anxiety disorder who received a session of ImRs reported a more positive and less intense emotional response to the retrieval of the memory, as well as a reduction in the perceived validity and accuracy of the negative memory-related beliefs about the self compared to participants in the control (no intervention) condition. After the intervention, most of their participants revised the content of the memory-associated beliefs, reporting more benign ones.

Taken together, the findings summarised above suggest that cognitive-behavioural interventions such as PE and ImRs can have a significant impact on how the targeted AMs subsequently affect individuals. These interventions seem to help patients access adverse memories in detail, reduce the memories' negative affective charge, and modify the beliefs or self-images that individuals may have developed as a result of these memories. As mentioned in Chapter 4, the ability to access specific AMs associated with positive affect and positive adaptive meanings could be an indicator of a healthy narrative identity and memory system (Singer, Blagov, Berry, & Oost, 2013). Interventions such as PE, IR, and ImRs, therefore, may help individuals develop or restore a healthy narrative identity. The literature on the memory-self relationship and narrative identity may thus provide additional information that can help us understand how these interventions work.

Understanding cognitive-behavioural interventions from a narrative identity perspective

Several researchers (e.g., Adler, 2012; McAdams & McLean, 2013; Singer, 2005; Singer et al., 2013) have argued that psychotherapy helps individuals to make sense of their experiences, incorporate lessons and insights from these experiences into their sense of self, develop a sense of agency and redemption, and construct a coherent narrative identity. It can thus help patients "re-story their lives" (McAdams & McLean, 2013, p. 235). Some evidence on patients' narratives about therapy and its impact on the self suggests that during treatment enhanced meaning making is associated with improvements in mental health (see Adler, 2012; Adler, Harmeling, & Walder-Biesanz, 2013). Recently, O'Toole, Watson, Rosenberg, and Berntsen (2018) reported that patients with social anxiety disorder and panic disorder rated negative (anxiety-related) AMs as less central for their identity and life story after CBT compared to before. This change was marginally greater in patients who experienced reliable change in their symptoms and occurred even though there was no explicit focus on memory in the treatment protocol. These findings suggest that CBT could affect the perception of memories even when they are not a treatment target. These shifts may arise because CBT teaches patients to think more adaptively, evaluate and challenge their core beliefs (O'Toole et al., 2018), and set more adaptive goals. Modifying maladaptive beliefs that are directly related to AMs may help individuals spontaneously re-appraise these AMs and respond differently when they are activated (see O'Toole et al., 2018). Challenging these beliefs using specific positive experiences that contradict them could also help reduce overgeneral retrieval as individuals learn to use specific AMs to evaluate their beliefs (Sutherland & Bryant, 2007).

Although memory and the self are inextricably linked, self changes following CBT and their role in symptom reduction have not been studied systematically to date (Gregory et al., 2018). We would like to propose that the critical memories on which patients' negative self-beliefs are based should be conceptualised as self-defining memories (SDMs; see Chapter 2) and that combining these with the life story model of personality (e.g., McAdams, 2015) may offer a way to conceptualise and understand the impact of CBT on the self. The maladaptive beliefs at the centre of the generic cognitive model may represent negative self-event connections that have been constructed through the process of autobiographical reasoning and have become part of individuals' narrative identity and long-term self. As discussed in Chapter 2, the life story model proposes that the life story or narrative identity consists of the stories that individuals construct in order to make sense of their experiences and link their past, present, and future selves. The long-term self, proposed in the self-memory system (SMS) model (e.g., Conway, Singer, & Tagini, 2004), consists of individuals' autobiographical knowledge and conceptual knowledge about the self. When faced with adverse experiences that challenge their sense of self, individuals attempt to make sense of them and establish causal coherence in their life story through autobiographical reasoning (for a description of the different types of coherence, see Chapter 2). They may thus form negative connections between these experiences and their sense of self. Once they have done that, individuals may attempt to preserve the status quo of the SMS and the coherence of their life story. For example, they may try to establish thematic coherence in the life story by interpreting new experiences through the lens of the existing negative self-event connections. This is something that the cognitive model recognises as new information being assimilated into existing schemas (Beck & Dozois, 2011). Individuals may also attempt to achieve a sense of self-continuity by setting up adversity-related goals (e.g., *"I will never allow anyone to hurt me again"*) and future-oriented images of the self (e.g., *"I will always be lonely"*). Negative self-event connections and associated goals and self-images may thus become part of the long-term self. As such, they may be elicited at any time as part of the working self that is activated in response to internal or environmental stimuli (see Chapters 2 and 3). They can thus trigger maladaptive cognitive, affective, and behavioural reactions and contribute to patients' symptoms.

Using this framework and the existing evidence on CBT, it is reasonable to argue that cognitive-behavioural interventions targeting adverse SDMs through verbal evaluation and/or experiential techniques may promote change at each of the layers of personality proposed by McAdams (e.g., 2015): dispositional traits, goals and values, and life story. We propose that change may start from modifications happening at the life story level. First, as shown in Figure 5.1, cognitive-behavioural interventions targeting adverse memories may facilitate autobiographical reasoning as they help patients reappraise their negative experiences and make more benign connections between these experiences and their sense of self. Through components such as post-exposure processing in PE, targeting hotspots in IR, or rescripting from the current self and younger self perspective in ImRs, patients may shift from self-event connections such as *"I am vulnerable"* to *"I struggle sometimes, but overall I am strong and can cope with problems."* Treatment components such as intervening in the memory in IR and ImRs may enhance the sense of mastery and agency associated with these memories. Furthermore, these interventions may help patients create redemption narratives, for example *"Being bullied was horrible, but I have become stronger and more considerate of others because of it."* Given the affective nature of redemption (see Chapter 4), the memories targeted in treatment may thus acquire a more positive emotional tone. These changes may lead to patients achieving closure or what Pals (2006) calls *coherent positive resolution*: a narrative of their adverse experiences that ends positively and is associated with a sense of resolution and being able to move on. They may also affect the rest of the life story as patients attempt to link the "resolved" memory to other AMs and set out to re-establish causal and thematic coherence in the life story, this time from a more positive perspective. Ultimately, CBT focusing on SDMs may help patients achieve the sense of self-continuity and unity which, as we saw in Chapter 4, is crucial for psychological well-being.

Second, memory-focused cognitive-behavioural interventions can help patients develop more positive goals, which in turn can lead to more adaptive behaviours. As discussed in Chapter 4, sometimes individuals set unrealistic goals related to their adverse experiences, depending on their interpretation of these experiences. Goals such as *"I must be 100% safe"* or *"I can never feel anxious"* often lead to maladaptive behaviours such as avoidance. These behaviours can deprive individuals of opportunities to experience positive events that might disconfirm some of their negative beliefs. CBT, by helping patients re-appraise their memories and the relationship between these memories and the self, may help patients to formulate more adaptive goals. Realistic goal setting can be an explicit focus of treatment, but it can also happen spontaneously. Brewin et al. (2009) found that some depressed patients experienced a decrease in rumination after ImRs, as well as spontaneous behavioural activation that allowed them to engage in positive activities. This happened despite the fact that treatment did not involve explicit attempts to modify behaviour. In this case, the change may have been

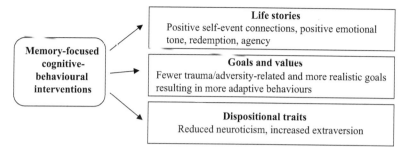

Figure 5.1 Proposed impact of memory-focused cognitive-behavioural interventions on each layer of personality.

due to changes in the life story. Indeed, creating redemptive stories can contribute to positive behavioural change (see Dunlop & Tracy, 2013).

Finally, as Figure 5.1 shows, cognitive-behavioural interventions targeting distressing SDMs may also affect individuals at the level of dispositional traits. Some evidence suggests that scores on certain personality traits, such as neuroticism and introversion, may decrease to a certain degree following therapy (see Zinbarg, Uliaszek, & Adler, 2008). Neuroticism has been associated with negative affect (Steel, Schmidt, & Schultz, 2008), avoidance motivation (Elliot & Thrash, 2002), greater contamination in the life story (Adler, Kissel, & McAdams, 2006), more negative life chapters (Thomsen, Olesen, Schnieber, & Tønnesvang, 2014), and fewer self-event connections referring to attitudes or perspectives about the world in SDMs (McLean & Fournier, 2008). Extraversion, on the other hand, is associated with positive affect (Steel et al., 2008), approach motivation (Elliot & Thrash, 2002), and more positive life chapters (Thomsen et al., 2014). It is thus possible to speculate that more positive AMs and life chapters, more positive self-views and insights, and reduced avoidance might be associated with reduced neuroticism and increased extraversion.

By effecting change at all personality levels, cognitive-behavioural interventions could modify how AMs targeted in treatment exert their self and directive functions in the long run. This change is likely to be associated with a change in how the modified AMs exert their functions on a daily basis. More positive self-event connections could contribute to the development or strengthening of working selves containing more adaptive self-images and goals. When these working selves are activated in response to the retrieval of the targeted AMs or images, they may elicit less negative and more positive affect, more positive self-evaluations, and more adaptive behaviours. As discussed in Chapter 4, the frequent experience of positive self-evaluations may contribute to an increase in self-esteem. The frequent experience of more positive affect, on the other hand, may contribute to greater flexibility and more efficient behaviour and problem solving. By modifying the meanings associated with memories and intrusive images, as well as the reactions they elicit upon retrieval, memory-focused cognitive-behavioural interventions may thus modify the way in which these AMs and images exert – or are used for – self and directive functions.

Some preliminary evidence for the above argument comes from a pilot study (Çili, Pettit, & Stopa, 2017) in which we administered one session of ImRs to 20 participants. Participants rescripted a negative SDM that still troubled them and we assessed their reactions to the retrieval of this memory before and after the ImRs session. Results showed that, one week after the ImRs session, participants rated their memory as less negative, less distressing, and less important for their sense of self than prior to rescripting. They also reported reductions in the belief associated with their memory, which we had elicited with the questions: *"In what ways do you think this experience has influenced you? What does the memory say about you as a person? Does it say anything about other people / the world in general?"* After recalling their SDM at the one-week follow-up, participants also reported higher state self-esteem and positive affect and lower negative affect than they did after recalling it in the first session. These changes may have been due to the activation of working selves containing self-images and goals that were relevant to the memory but had been modified or – if we rely on Brewin's (2006) hypothesis – due to the activation of new or newly strengthened positive working selves. Ours was a pilot study with a small non-clinical sample and no control condition, so the findings need to be treated with caution. However, they suggest that ImRs may attenuate the impact of the rescripted memory's retrieval on affect and self-evaluations.

Using the narrative identity literature to inform cognitive-behavioural interventions

Our attempt to understand the generic cognitive model and CBT in terms of the narrative identity literature is not an exercise that simply aims to bring together different strands of literature. We believe that the framework provided by the life story model and the growing evidence on narrative identity and well-being can not only give us a better understanding of how CBT works, but can also help us enhance it. In particular, we believe that the literature we have presented in this book can help therapists increase their understanding of patients' difficulties and take a broader perspective of their life story when planning and administering treatment.

First, in line with Singer (e.g., Singer, 2005, 2006; Singer et al., 2013) and Zinbarg et al. (2008), we propose that drawing on the personality and AM literature could enhance therapists' understanding of their patients' difficulties by providing a more nuanced account of how previous experience contributes to and maintains psychological problems. The focus on modifying maladaptive behaviours and, in some cases, core beliefs in CBT may sometimes mean that the broader picture of patients' life story and overall personality is missed. Taking a broader perspective using McAdams' (e.g., 2015) model, on the other hand, can indicate how patients got to their current state. Assessing personality traits, for example, can help therapists understand how patients think, feel, and behave (Zinbarg et al., 2008) and how they process and organise their AMs. This is important since individuals who score low in openness to experience may not be particularly likely to explore memories and their meanings (see Lilgendahl & McAdams, 2011; Lodi-Smith, Geise, & Roberts, 2009), whereas individuals who score low in conscientiousness may struggle to create coherent narratives or make growth-related self-event connections (Lodi-Smith et al., 2009; McLean & Fournier, 2008). Similarly, understanding how the life story develops thanks to autobiographical reasoning and the need for the life story to be temporally, causally, and thematically coherent can supplement the cognitive model's arguments regarding schematic processing of information (Beck & Dozois, 2011). It can thus help therapists understand how negative beliefs develop and how they can affect the entire life story, as individuals engage in misguided attempts to preserve a coherent sense of self. Asking patients about their SDMs, on the other hand, can help therapists understand what matters to these patients and what functions these SDMs play in their lives (Singer, 2006).

Second, cognitive-behavioural therapists can use the narrative identity literature in treatment. For some patients it may be helpful to provide psychoeducation about memory functions and train them to identify and use SDMs for adaptive purposes (e.g., mood repair) in difficult situations (Singer, 2006). Similarly, therapists can educate patients about working self shifts following SDM retrieval and train them to manipulate working self activation and deliberately access more positive working selves when negative SDMs are retrieved (Çili & Stopa, 2015). They can also educate patients about autobiographical reasoning and how they can use it to attribute more positive meanings to their experiences. Furthermore, therapists can incorporate treatment elements focusing on patients' broader life story into their clinical practice. As discussed in Chapter 4, it is important for individuals to have positive coherent chapters and life stories in general. It is also important for them to establish a sense of self-continuity. For some patients, working on a few AMs during treatment may not be sufficient. If they have held on to these memories and their meanings for a long time and have established a coherent but negative view of themselves, a change in the memories may temporarily threaten their self-continuity. Alternatively, for traumatic memories that threatened self-continuity to begin with, therapeutic work may need a greater focus on linking these memories to the rest of patients' autobiographical knowledge. Although the skills patients learn in CBT may generalise to how they make sense of their experiences outside the therapy room (O'Toole et al., 2008), this is not always the case. For patients with complex difficulties and multiple traumatic experiences, it might be necessary to explicitly help with the integration and restoration of self-continuity. This could be achieved by combining CBT with elements of interventions that focus on the life story.

Interventions that may inform traditional CBT include narrative exposure therapy (NET), life review, and life-review therapy. NET is a fairly recent cognitive-behavioural intervention that was originally developed for helping survivors of war and organised violence (Schauer, Neuner, & Elbert, 2011). It involves exposure to the traumatic experiences followed by attempts to place these experiences into the context of one's life in order to develop a temporally coherent life narrative. This is often achieved by patients creating a chronological timeline of their life using a rope and objects (e.g., flowers, stones) representing positive and negative significant memories (see Mørkved et al., 2014). Life review interventions also involve a review of major positive and negative life events. They aim to promote the use of AMs and reminiscence for positive functions such as problem solving (Westerhof, Bohlmeijer, & Webster, 2010). In life review, individuals are encouraged to review their life and resolve past conflicts while evaluating the significance and impact of their experiences (Bohlmeijer, Roemer, Cuijpers, & Smit, 2007; Westerhof et al., 2010). The focus is on reviewing positive and negative AMs from across the life course and helping individuals acknowledge what they have learnt from these memories and how they have become the person they are. This intervention may contribute to the development of a sense of self-continuity and purpose and promote the use of AMs for problem solving and identity construction (Bohlmeijer et al., 2007; Westerhof et al., 2010). Life-review therapy is similar to life review, but it may be used with individuals experiencing more serious psychological issues, such as anxiety and depression (see Westerhof et al., 2010).

Overall, evidence suggests that life review and life-review therapy are effective in alleviating symptoms of depression and enhancing psychological well-being (Bohlmeijer et al., 2007; Pinquart & Forstmeier, 2012; Westerhof et al., 2010), although they may not necessarily be superior to other established interventions (see Hitchcock et al., 2017). Similarly, NET can be effective in addressing PTSD symptoms, although more research is needed (for reviews, see Mørkved et al., 2014; Robjant & Fazel, 2010). According to Maercker and Bachem (2013), the effectiveness of life review interventions may be due to the balanced review of positive and negative life experiences (although the aim is to make positive experiences more salient), the elaboration and detailed recall of AMs, and attributing meaning to these AMs. These interventions, just like the NET, may enable individuals to recall specific AMs and to create positive connections between these AMs and the self. The fact that they are simple yet effective suggests that at least some of their elements can be incorporated into CBT practice. Following IR or ImRs, for example, therapists may discuss with patients how the modified AMs fit with the rest of their life story and how they may be linked to other memories in order to establish a sense of self-continuity and unity of the self. Of course, some CBT therapists may already be doing this, albeit under a different name. We also need further research in order to determine whether there is a need to incorporate life review techniques in standard CBT, when this need may arise, and whether approaches incorporating life review are likely to be superior to the use of CBT focusing only on particular AMs (e.g., in preventing relapse). The effectiveness of interventions focusing on the life story, however, is promising.

Conclusion

In this chapter, we focused on how CBT conceptualises psychopathology and how it addresses distressing AMs and intrusive images using verbal cognitive evaluation and experiential techniques. We argued that, although CBT is currently considered to be the gold standard of psychotherapy, it is not always effective and does not always prevent relapse. We proposed that one way to enhance CBT and particular cognitive-behavioural techniques is to first obtain a better understanding of how they work. We argued that changes in the memory-self relationship that result either directly or indirectly from CBT can be understood from a narrative identity perspective that involves all three layers of personality: the life story or narrative identity, goals and values, and dispositional traits. By experiencing changes in each of these layers as a result of treatment, individuals can achieve a more positive and coherent life story, a sense of self-continuity, and a sense of purpose that involves more adaptive goals. These changes may then contribute to symptom alleviation. Our theory highlights the need for therapists to understand and place greater emphasis on the role that adverse AMs play in patients' life story, as well as the need for further research on the outcomes of CBT. We make recommendations for future research in the final chapter of this book.

References

Adler, J. M. (2012). Living into the story: Agency and coherence in a longi-tudinal study of narrative identity development and mental health over the course of psychotherapy. *Journal of Personality and Social Psychology, 102*(2), 367–389.

Adler, J. M., Harmeling, L. H., & Walder-Biesanz, I. (2013). Narrative meaning making is associated with sudden gains in psychotherapy clients' mental health under routine clinical conditions. *Journal of Consulting and Clinical Psychology, 81*(5), 839–845.

Adler, J. M., Kissel, E. C., & McAdams, D. P. (2006). Emerging from the CAVE: Attributional style and the narrative study of identity in midlife adults. *Cognitive Therapy and Research, 30*(1), 39–51.

Arntz, A. (2011). Imagery rescripting for personality disorders. *Cognitive and Behavioral Practice, 18*, 466–481.

Arntz, A., Sofi, D., & van Breukelen, G. (2013). Imagery Rescripting as treatment for complicated PTSD in refugees: A multiple baseline case series study. *Behaviour Research and Therapy, 51*, 274–283.

Arntz, A., Tiesema, M., & Kindt, M. (2007). Treatment of PTSD: A com-parison of imaginal exposure with and without imagery rescripting. *Journal of Behavior Therapy and Experimental Psychiatry, 38*, 345–370.

Arntz, A. & Weertman, A. (1999). Treatment of childhood memories: Theory and practice. *Behaviour Research and Therapy, 37*, 715–740.

Beck, A. T. (1967). *Depression: Causes and treatment*. Philadelphia, PA: University of Pennsylvania Press.

Beck, A. T. & Dozois, D. J. (2011). Cognitive therapy: Current status and future directions. *Annual Review of Medicine, 62*, 397–409.

Beck, A. T., Emery, G., & Greenberg, R. L. (1985). *Anxiety disorders and phobias: A cognitive perspective*. New York, NY: Basic Books.

Beck, A. T., Rush, A. J., Shaw, B. F., & Emery, G. (1979). *Cognitive therapy of depression*. New York, NY: Guilford Press.

Beck, J. S. (2011). *Cognitive behavior therapy: Basics and beyond (2nd ed.)*. New York, NY: Guilford Press.

Bohlmeijer, E., Roemer, M., Cuijpers, P., & Smit, F. (2007). The effects of rem-iniscence on psychological well-being in older adults: A meta-analysis. *Aging & Mental Health, 11*(3), 291–300.

Brewin, C. R. (2006). Understanding cognitive behaviour therapy: A retrieval competition account. *Behaviour Research and Therapy, 44,* 765–784.

Brewin, C. R., Gregory, J. D., Lipton, M., & Burgess, N. (2010). Intrusive images in psychological disorders: Characteristics, neural mechanisms, and treatment implications. *Psychological Review, 117,* 210–232.

Brewin, C. R., Wheatley, J., Patel, T., Fearon, P., Hackmann, A., et al. (2009). Imagery rescripting as a brief stand-alone treatment for depressed patients with intrusive memories. *Behaviour Research and Therapy, 47,* 569–576.

Butler, A. C., Chapman, J. E., Forman, E. M., & Beck, A. T. (2006). The empirical status of cognitive-behavioral therapy: A review of meta-analyses. *Clinical Psychology Review, 26*(1), 17–31.

Çili, S., Pettit, S., & Stopa, L. (2017). Impact of imagery rescripting on adverse self-defining memories and post-recall working selves in a non-clinical sample: A pilot study. *Cognitive Behaviour Therapy, 46*(1), 75–89.

Çili, S. & Stopa, L. (2015). The retrieval of self-defining memories is associated with the activation of specific working selves. *Memory, 23*(2), 233–253.

Clark, D. M. (2001). A cognitive perspective on social phobia. In W. R. Crozier & L. E. Alden (Eds.), *International handbook of social anxiety: Concepts, research, and interventions relating to the self and shyness* (pp. 405–430). Chichester, England: John Wiley & Sons.

Clark, D. M. & Wells, A. (1995). A cognitive model of social phobia. In R. G. Heimberg, M. R. Liebowitz, D. A. Hope, & F. R. Schneier (Eds.), *Social phobia: Diagnosis, assessment, and treatment* (pp. 69–93). New York, NY: Guilford Press.

Conway, M. A., Singer, J. A., & Tagini, A. (2004). The self and autobiographical memory: Correspondence and coherence. *Social Cognition, 22*(5), 491–529.

Cooper, A. A., Clifton, E. G., & Feeny, N. C. (2017). An empirical review of potential mediators and mechanisms of prolonged exposure therapy. *Clinical Psychology Review, 56,* 106–121.

Cooper, M. J., Wells, A., & Todd, G. (2004). A cognitive model of bulimia nervosa. *British Journal of Clinical Psychology, 43,* 1–16.

Dalgleish, T. & Werner-Seidler, A. (2014). Disruptions in autobiographical memory processing in depression and the emergence of memory therapeutics. *Trends in Cognitive Sciences, 18*(11), 596–604.

David, D., Cristea, I., & Hofmann, S. G. (2018). Why cognitive behavioral therapy is the current gold standard of psychotherapy. *Frontiers in Psychiatry, 9,* 4.

Dibbets, P. & Arntz, A. (2016). Imagery rescripting: Is incorporation of the most aversive scenes necessary? *Memory, 24*(5), 683–695.

Dunlop, W. L. & Tracy, J. L. (2013). Sobering stories: Narratives of self-redemption predict behavioral change and improved health among recovering alcoholics. *Journal of Personality and Social Psychology, 104*(3), 576–590.

Edwards, D. (2007). Restructuring implicational meaning through memory-based imagery: Some historical notes. *Journal of Behavior Therapy and Experimental Psychiatry, 38*(4), 306–316.

Ehlers, A. & Clark, D. M. (2000). A cognitive model of posttraumatic stress disorder. *Behaviour Research and Therapy, 38*, 319–345.

Ehlers, A. & Clark, D. M. (2008). Post-traumatic stress disorder: The development of effective psychological treatments. *Nordic Journal of Psychiatry, 62*, 11–18.

Ehlers, A., Clark, D. M., Hackmann, A., McManus, F., & Fennell, M. (2005). Cognitive therapy for post-traumatic stress disorder: Development and evaluation. *Behaviour Research and Therapy, 43*(4), 413–431.

Elliot, A. J. & Thrash, T. M. (2002). Approach-avoidance motivation in personality: Approach and avoidance temperaments and goals. *Journal of Personality and Social Psychology, 82*(5), 804–818.

Elliott, R., Watson, J. C., Goldman, R. N., & Greenberg, L. S. (2004). *Learning emotion-focused therapy: The process-experiential approach to change.* Washington, DC: American Psychological Association.

Fang, A., Sawyer, A. T., Asnaani, A., & Hofmann, S. G. (2013). Social mishap exposures for social anxiety disorder: An important treatment ingredient. *Cognitive and Behavioral Practice, 20*(2), 213–220.

Foa, E. B. & Kozak, M. J. (1986). Emotional processing of fear: Exposure to corrective information. *Psychological Bulletin, 99*(1), 20–35.

Foa, E. B., Rothbaum, B. O., Riggs, D. S., & Murdock, T. B. (1991). Treatment of posttraumatic stress disorder in rape victims: A comparison between cognitive-behavioral procedures and counseling. *Journal of Consulting and Clinical Psychology, 59*(5), 715–723.

Frets, P. G., Kevenaar, C., & van der Heiden, C. (2014). Imagery rescripting as a stand-alone treatment for patients with social phobia: A case series. *Journal of Behavior Therapy and Experimental Psychiatry, 45*(1), 160–169.

Gregory, B. & Peters, L. (2017). Changes in the self during cognitive behavioural therapy for social anxiety disorder: A systematic review. *Clinical Psychology Review, 52*, 1–18.

Gregory, B., Wong, Q. J. J., Marker, C. D., & Peters, L. (2018). Maladaptive self-beliefs during cognitive behavioural therapy for social anxiety disorder: A test of temporal precedence. *Cognitive Therapy and Research, 42*(3), 261–272.

Grunnert, B. K., Smucker, M. R., Weis, J. M., & Rusch, M. D. (2003). When prolonged exposure fails: Adding an imagery-based cognitive restructuring component in the treatment of industrial accident victims suffering from PTSD. *Cognitive and Behavioral Practice, 10*(4), 333–346.

Hackmann, A., Ehlers, A., Speckens, A., & Clark, D. M. (2004). Characteristics and content of intrusive memories in PTSD and their changes with treatment. *Journal of Traumatic Stress, 17*(3), 231–240.

Hirsch, C. R. & Mathews, A. (2012). A cognitive model of pathological worry. *Behaviour Research and Therapy, 50*(10), 636–646.

Hitchcock, C., Werner-Seidler, A., Blackwell, S. E., & Dalgleish, T. (2017). Autobiographical episodic memory-based training for the treatment of mood, anxiety and stress-related disorders: A systematic review and meta-analysis. *Clinical Psychology Review, 52*, 92–107.

Hofmann, S. G., Asnaani, A., Vonk, I. J. J., Sawyer, A. T., & Fang, A. (2012). The efficacy of cognitive behavioral therapy: A review of meta-analyses. *Cognitive Therapy and Research, 36*(5), 427–440.

Holmes, E. A., Arntz, A., & Smucker, M. R. (2007). Imagery rescripting in cognitive behaviour therapy: Images, treatment techniques and outcomes. *Journal of Behavior Therapy and Experimental Psychiatry, 38*(4), 297–305.

Ison, R., Medoro, L., Keen, N., & Kuipers, E. (2014). The use of rescripting imagery for people with psychosis who hear voices. *Behavioural and Cognitive Psychotherapy, 42*(2), 129–142.

Langkaas, T. F., Hoffart, A., Øktedalen, T., Ulvenes, P. G., Hembree, E. A., & Smucker, M. (2017). Exposure and non-fear emotions: A randomized controlled study of exposure-based and rescripting-based imagery in PTSD treatment. *Behaviour Research and Therapy, 97*, 33–42.

Lee, S. W. & Kwon, J. H. (2013). The efficacy of imagery rescripting (IR) for social phobia: A randomized controlled trial. *Journal of Behavior Therapy and Experimental Psychiatry, 44*(4), 351–360.

Lilgendahl, J. P. & McAdams, D. P. (2011). Constructing stories of self-growth: How individual differences in patterns of autobiographical reasoning relate to well-being in midlife. *Journal of Personality, 79*(2), 391–428.

Lodi-Smith, J., Geise, A. C., Roberts, B. W., & Robins, R. W. (2009). Narrating personality change. *Journal of Personality and Social Psychology, 96*(3), 679–689.

Lynch, D., Laws, K. R., & McKenna, P. J. (2010). Cognitive behavioural therapy for major psychiatric disorder: Does it really work? A meta-analytical review of well-controlled trials. *Psychological Medicine, 40*(1), 9–24.

Maercker, A. & Bachem, R. (2013). Life-review interventions as psycho-therapeutic techniques in psychotraumatology. *European Journal of Psychotraumatology, 4*(1), 19720.

McAdams, D. P. (2015). Three lines of personality development: A conceptual itinerary. *European Psychologist, 20*(4), 252–264.

McAdams, D. P. & McLean, K. C. (2013). Narrative identity. *Current Directions in Psychological Science, 22*(3), 233–238.

McLean, C. P. & Foa, E. B. (2011). Prolonged exposure therapy for post-traumatic stress disorder: A review of evidence and dissemination. *Expert Review of Neurotherapeutics, 11*(8), 1151–1163.

McLean, K. C. & Fournier, M. A. (2008). The content and processes of autobiographical reasoning in narrative identity. *Journal of Research in Personality, 42*(3), 527–545.

Morina, N., Lancee, J., & Arntz, A. (2017). Imagery rescripting as a clinical intervention for aversive memories: A meta-analysis. *Journal of Behavior Therapy and Experimental Psychiatry, 55*, 6–15.

Mørkved, N., Hartmann, K., Aarsheim, L. M., Holen, D., Milde, A. M., et al. (2014). A comparison of narrative exposure therapy and prolonged exposure therapy for PTSD. *Clinical Psychology Review, 34*(6), 453–467.

Nilsson, J.-E., Lundh, L.-G., & Viborg, G. (2012). Imagery rescripting of early memories in social anxiety disorder: An experimental study. *Behaviour Research and Therapy, 50*(6), 387–392.

Øktedalen, T., Hoffart, A., & Langkaas, T. F. (2015). Trauma-related shame and guilt as time-varying predictors of posttraumatic stress disorder symptoms during imagery exposure and imagery rescripting: A randomized controlled trial. *Psychotherapy Research, 25*(5), 518–532.

O'Toole, M. S., Watson, L., Rosenberg, N. K., & Berntsen, D. (2018). Changes in perceived centrality of anxious events following cognitive behavioral therapy for social anxiety disorder and panic disorder. *Journal of Behavior Therapy and Experimental Psychiatry, 59*, 150–156.

Padesky, C. A. (1994). Schema change processes in cognitive therapy. *Clinical Psychology and Psychotherapy, 1*(5), 267–278.

Pals, J. L. (2006). Narrative identity processing of difficult life experiences: Pathways of personality development and positive self-transformation in adulthood. *Journal of Personality, 74*(4), 1079–1110.

Pinquart, M. & Forstmeier, S. (2012). Effects of reminiscence interventions on psychosocial outcomes: A meta-analysis. *Aging & Mental health, 16*(5), 541–558.

Powers, M. B., Halpern, J. M., Ferenschak, M. P., Gillihan, S. J., & Foa, E. B. (2010). A meta-analytic review of prolonged exposure for posttraumatic stress disorder. *Clinical Psychology Review, 30*(6), 635–641.

Raabe, S., Ehring, T., Marquenie, L., Olff, M., & Kindt, M. (2015). Imagery rescripting as stand-alone treatment for posttraumatic stress disorder related to childhood abuse. *Journal of Behavior Therapy and Experimental Psychiatry, 48*, 170–176.

Reimer, S. G., & Moscovitch, D. A. (2015). The impact of imagery rescripting on memory appraisals and core beliefs in social anxiety disorder. *Behaviour Research and Therapy, 75*, 48–59.

Ritter, V. & Stangier, U. (2016). Seeing in the Mind's eye: Imagery rescripting for patients with body dysmorphic disorder. A single case series. *Journal of Behavior Therapy and Experimental Psychiatry, 50*, 187–195.

Robjant, K. & Fazel, M. (2010). The emerging evidence for narrative exposure therapy: A review. *Clinical Psychology Review, 30*(8), 1030–1039.

Schauer, M., Neuner, F., & Elbert, T. (2011). *Narrative exposure therapy: A short-term treatment for traumatic stress disorders (2nd ed.)*. Cambridge, MA: Hogrefe Publishing.

Singer, J. A. (2005). *Personality and psychotherapy: Treating the whole person.* New York, NY: Guilford Press.

Singer, J. A. (2006). Memory, emotion, and psychotherapy: Maximizing the positive functions of self-defining memories. In R. Uttl, N. Ohta, & A. Siegenthaler (Eds.), *Memory and emotion: Interdisciplinary perspectives* (pp. 211–232). Oxford, England: Blackwell Publishing.

Singer, J. A., Blagov, P., Berry, M., & Oost, K. M. (2013). Self-defining memories, scripts, and the life story: Narrative identity in personality and psychotherapy. *Journal of Personality, 81*(6), 569–582.

Singer, J. A. & Salovey, P. (1993). *The remembered self: Emotion and memory in personality.* New York, NY: Free Press.

Smucker, M. R., Dancu, C., Foa, E. B., & Niederee, J. L. (1995). Imagery rescripting: A new treatment for survivors of childhood sexual abuse suffering from posttraumatic stress. *Journal of Cognitive Psychotherapy: An International Quarterly, 9*(1), 3–17.

Smucker, M. R. & Niederee, J. (1995). Treating incest-related PTSD and pathogenic schemas through imaginal exposure and rescripting. *Cognitive and Behavioral Practice, 2*(1), 63–93.

Steel, P., Schmidt, J., & Shultz, J. (2008). Refining the relationship between personality and subjective well-being. *Psychological Bulletin, 134*(1), 138–161.

Stopa, L. (2009). How to use imagery in cognitive-behavioural therapy. In L. Stopa (Ed.), *Imagery and the threatened self: Perspectives on mental imagery and the self in cognitive therapy* (pp. 65–93). London, England: Routledge.

Sutherland, K. & Bryant, R. A. (2007). Autobiographical memory in posttraumatic stress disorder before and after treatment. *Behaviour Research and Therapy, 45*(12), 2915–2923.

Thoma, N. C. & McKay, D. (Eds.) (2015). *Working with emotion in cognitive-behavioural therapy: Techniques for clinical practice.* New York, NY: Guilford Press.

Thomsen, D. K., Olesen, M. H., Schnieber, A., & Tønnesvang, J. (2014). The emotional content of life stories: Positivity bias and relation to personality. *Cognition and Emotion, 28*(2), 260–277.

Veale, D., Page, N., Woodward, E., & Salkovskis, P. (2015). Imagery rescripting for obsessive compulsive disorder: A single case experimental design in 12 cases. *Journal of Behavior Therapy and Experimental Psychiatry, 49*, 230–236.

Weertman, A. & Arntz, A. (2007). Effectiveness of treatment of childhood memories in cognitive therapy for personality disorders: A controlled study contrasting methods focusing on the present and methods focusing on childhood memories. *Behaviour Research and Therapy, 45*(9), 2133–2143.

Westerhof, G. J., Bohlmeijer, E., & Webster, J. D. (2010). Reminiscence and mental health: A review of recent progress in theory, research and interventions. *Ageing & Society, 30*(4), 697–721.

Wild, J., Hackmann, A., & Clark, D. M. (2007). When the present visits the past: Updating traumatic memories in social phobia. *Journal of Behavior Therapy and Experimental Psychiatry, 38*(4), 386–401.

Wild, J., Hackmann, A., & Clark, D. M. (2008). Rescripting early memories linked to negative images in social phobia: A pilot study. *Behavior Therapy, 39*(1), 47–56.

Willson, R., Veale, D., & Freeston, M. (2016). Imagery rescripting for body dysmorphic disorder: A multiple-baseline single-case experimental design. *Behavior Therapy, 47*(2), 248–261.

Young, J. E. (1999). *Cognitive therapy for personality disorders: A schema-focused approach (3rd ed.).* Sarasota, FL: Professional Resource Press.

Zinbarg, R. E., Uliaszek, A. A., & Adler, J. M. (2008). The role of personality in psychotherapy for anxiety and depression. *Journal of Personality, 76*(6), 1649–1688.

6 What next? Reflections and directions for future research on the memory-self relationship

Introduction

We started this book with the story of Sir Ian McKellen returning a rumoured £1 million advance for his memoirs because "It was a bit painful. I didn't want to go back into my life and imagine things that I hadn't understood so far" (Oppenheim, 2016). This decision was understandable given the powerful role that autobiographical memories (AMs) play in our lives. As we have shown in the preceding chapters, AM functions as a sort of multi-purpose tool which helps us manage our behaviour, make decisions and plans, solve problems, build interpersonal relationships, and develop a sense of self (Chapter 1). We use it as we engage in autobiographical reasoning to learn lessons from our experiences; draw conclusions about ourselves; and construct a story about our lives that links our past, present, and future selves and gives us a sense of purpose (Chapter 2). AMs can also affect our emotions, behaviours, and perceptions of ourselves when we recall them, potentially because they lead to the activation of related working selves which guide cognition, affect, and behaviour as we adapt to our environment (Chapter 3). Occasionally, the multi-purpose tool can malfunction. Adverse AMs associated with intense negative affect, negative meanings, and an overgeneral or intrusive pattern of retrieval can contribute to the onset and maintenance of psychological disorders by giving rise to maladaptive behaviours and negative beliefs (Chapter 4). Such AMs are often (but not always) targeted in cognitive-behavioural therapy (CBT), which uses verbal evaluation and experiential techniques to modify their meanings and reduce their emotional intensity (Chapter 5).

As we stated earlier, our aim in writing this book was to synthesise existing literature on the memory-self relationship and its clinical relevance and to encourage further interdisciplinary research. Having reviewed the key literature, in this final chapter we turn our attention to some current issues and debates in the field. Some of these (e.g., the nature of trauma memories) are issues that we have referred to earlier in the book. Others are related to recent developments, such as the use of visuospatial tasks and pharmacological interventions to alter adverse memories and their consequences. After summarising these issues, we propose directions for further research.

Reflections on current issues and debates in AM research

As we have highlighted throughout this book, there is now a significant body of literature on AM. Nevertheless, there are still issues that need to be addressed by researchers if we are to obtain a better understanding of memory, its relationship to psychological well-being, and memory-focused therapeutic interventions. We believe that among the issues that need to be prioritised are the definition and assessment of meaning making, the nature of trauma memories, mechanisms of change in CBT, and novel interventions involving memory manipulation.

In Chapter 4, we mentioned that narrative identity literature often presents issues related to construct definition and assessment. One of these issues concerns meaning making, which is conceptualised in different ways in the literature (see Adler, Lodi-Smith, Philippe, & Houle, 2016; Park, 2010). It is usually assessed by reading memory narratives and coding self-event connections or statements indicating that individuals are reflecting on lessons learnt or on how their experience illustrates enduring or changed aspects of the self (e.g., McLean & Fournier, 2008; Singer & Blagov, 2000). As we saw in Chapters 2 and 4, however, there are multiple methods for coding AM narratives. This makes it difficult to ascertain whether different narrative indices (e.g., integrative meaning and narrative structure) overlap or assess distinct narrative qualities and to understand whether some indicators of meaning are more important for well-being than others (Graci, Watts, & Fivush, 2018). Furthermore, recently some researchers (e.g., Holm & Thomsen, 2018) have asked individuals to rate whether self-event connections in their life story indicate positive or negative characteristics of themselves or positive or negative self-change. Although this assessment method is promising and less time consuming for researchers, it may yield different results compared to coding. This discrepancy may be due to factors such as the potential ability of coding to capture meanings or narrative features that individuals are not aware of, as well as individuals' lack of interest in or limited time for elaborating on meanings in memory narratives (see Alea, 2018; Holm & Thomsen, 2018; Panattoni & McLean, 2018). At the moment, researchers (e.g., Holm & Thomsen,

2018; Panattoni & McLean, 2018) are recommending the use of self-ratings as a supplement to narrative coding. However, as Panattoni and McLean (2018) point out, it is important to understand the discrepancies between these assessment methods because they have implications for our understanding of narrative identity and for applied settings in which narrative change is important. A better understanding of meaning making can help us understand nuances in its relationship with well-being and thus inform therapeutic interventions which involve modification of meanings attached to AMs.

Another issue in the literature concerns trauma memories. As discussed in Chapter 4, there is an ongoing debate with regards to whether trauma memories are narratively coherent or fragmented and disorganised (see Brewin, 2016; Rubin, Berntsen, Ogle, Deffler, & Beckham, 2016). Although these memories have been found to be fragmented and disorganised in some cases, to date research findings are inconclusive (see Brewin, 2016; Berntsen & Rubin, 2014; Crespo & Fernández-Lansac, 2016). This is an important issue because it affects our understanding of trauma memories and how they should be targeted in therapy. A better understanding of these memories, especially of their structural narrative elements as defined in narrative identity literature (see Chapter 4), can enhance our understanding of the relationship between their characteristics and distress. Furthermore, it can inform interventions that focus on these memories, for example by helping clinicians identify when additional interventions are needed to enhance the coherence of trauma narratives and their integration with patients' life story.

An enhanced understanding of trauma memories or less severe negative memories is also relevant for our understanding of the mechanisms of change in cognitive-behavioural interventions targeting such memories. In Chapter 5, we presented several explanations for how techniques such as prolonged exposure and imagery rescripting (ImRs) might work, including modification in memory-related beliefs and meanings and a reduction in the emotional response to memory retrieval. We mentioned the arguments on whether CBT in general functions by modifying the structure or the accessibility of maladaptive schemas or self-representations. We also proposed that techniques targeting adverse memories might produce change at different levels of personality, including the life story, goals and values, and traits. So far, however, ours remains a hypothesis and clinical research has focused primarily on symptom-related outcomes of CBT. It is partly for this reason that CBT is sometimes characterised as taking a mechanistic perspective by focusing on "malfunctioning" aspects of individuals (e.g., beliefs, behaviours) rather than a holistic perspective (see Singer, 2005). However, the fact that to date the changes CBT produces in individuals' personality and sense of self have not been studied systematically (Gregory, Wong, Marker, & Peters, 2018) does not mean that they do not occur. As O'Toole, Watson, Rosenberg, and Berntsen (2018) found, individuals' perceptions of the relevance of adverse AMs for their identity and life story may change even if CBT does not particularly focus on these AMs. The debate on how exactly CBT works, therefore, cannot be resolved unless we have robust evidence on whether and how it affects individuals' life story, personality as a whole, and their sense of self. Resolving this debate is important. If we know what cognitive-behavioural interventions do and do not do, we can identify ways in which we can enhance them to ensure that patients experience positive lasting changes.

The question on how specific interventions work also applies to recent developments in clinical psychology. Two key developments are the use of visuospatial tasks such as Tetris for reducing intrusive imagery following trauma and the use of pharmacological agents such as propranolol for reducing the affective charge of fear/trauma memories. The use of tasks such as Tetris after the retrieval of key aspects of the trauma aims to disrupt the consolidation of the trauma memory immediately or soon after the trauma has occurred. It is thought to achieve this by competing for cognitive resources with the consolidation of the memory's sensory components while the memory is still malleable (see Iyadurai et al., 2018). Tetris has proved to be effective in reducing intrusions when used immediately after a motor vehicle accident (Iyadurai et al., 2018) and in women after an emergency Caesarean section (Horsch et al., 2017). In laboratory settings, it has also shown some promise in reducing intrusions for memories which had already been consolidated (e.g., Hagenaars, Holmes, Klaassen, & Elzinga, 2017). Similarly, interventions using propranolol aim to disrupt the consolidation or re-consolidation of adverse memories after they are retrieved and destabilised. Propranolol, which is a beta-blocker, may be administered before or after the reactivation of a memory (especially its peak emotional moments). To date, it has yielded promising results in reducing the memories' affective charge and thus dampening the emotional reactions to memory retrieval (see Beckers & Kindt, 2017; Elsey & Kindt, 2017; Kindt, 2018). However, as Kindt and her colleagues (e.g., Beckers & Kindt, 2017; Elsey & Kindt, 2017) acknowledge, the research on the use of agents such as propranolol in human participants is still limited, has produced inconsistent findings, and has targeted primarily recent fear memories that were not necessarily meaningful for participants (but see Kindt & van Emmerik, 2016). How it works and how it affects PTSD symptoms or memory characteristics other than affect remains unclear.

Our limited understanding of interventions involving Tetris and propranolol raises questions about their use. Some researchers have questioned the ethical implications of using technology to manipulate AMs (see Bluck, 2017; Westerhof, 2017). Although reconsolidation disruption – at least when involving propranolol – may not pose ethical issues because it does not seem to erase the memory itself (Beckers & Kindt, 2017), these researchers have queried the broader impact that this intervention may have on individuals' life story and sense of self. For example, Bluck (2017) argues that external manipulation of AMs (e.g., through propranolol) might make the memory system less adaptive in the face of new situations or tasks if it interferes with memory functions such as lesson learning. According to her, "when we consider tampering with memories, we face a balancing act between alleviating suffering and maintaining an individual's remembered past, their own unique life story, intact for future use" (Bluck, 2017, p. 6). In the absence of extensive empirical evidence on how interventions such as Tetris or propranolol affect individuals beyond intrusion or affect reduction, it is thus difficult to make claims about their effectiveness and usefulness or to make recommendations about their use in clinical settings. They are getting significant attention in the literature, possibly because they can produce change relatively quickly. Nevertheless, caution in using them is perhaps the best option for now.

Recommendations for future research

The issues highlighted above and in the preceding chapters indicate that there is a need to address and resolve important issues in the area of AM, the self, psychopathology, and CBT. Doing this can enable us to advance our understanding of these topics and enhance the practice of CBT. We propose that there are two important broad lines of enquiry that researchers need to follow: the involvement of AM in psychopathology and mechanisms of change in CBT and in new therapeutic interventions.

First, we believe that it is important to investigate further the relationship between AM and psychological well-being, as well as the involvement of AMs in psychological disorders. Despite the extensive body of work reviewed in Chapter 4, there are still questions that remain unanswered. For example, given the limited existing research in this area (see Adler et al., 2016), how relevant is the narrative structure of AMs (especially trauma memories) for psychological well-being and how can we best address it in therapy? What role do adverse AMs play in disorders that to date have not been studied extensively from a narrative identity perspective, for example eating disorders or dissociative disorders? What are the exact processes through which adverse AMs exert long-term and short-term effects on patients' sense of self, emotions, and behaviours? Are these processes transdiagnostic? Furthermore, we believe that it is important to understand the role of cultural and personality factors in memory processes in psychopathology. Culture can influence how we construct, narrate, interpret, and use our AMs (see Chapters 1 and 2); how we respond to memory retrieval (see Chapter 3); and how AMs affect well-being (see Chapter 4). Traits such as conscientiousness and neuroticism may also influence how we interpret and use our AMs (see Chapters 1 and 4). Understanding how these factors affect the memory-self relationship and its relevance for well-being can pave the way for better tailoring of memory-focused interventions to patients' needs.

Second, we believe that researchers need to make a greater use of the cognitive, personality, and social psychological literature to investigate mechanisms of change in CBT. As discussed in Chapter 5, and in line with Singer (2005), we propose that future research could draw on the life story model (e.g., McAdams, 2015) and narrative identity research methods to understand the changes promoted by specific cognitive-behavioural interventions such as ImRs. It can, for example, assess patients' personality traits and goals, the characteristics of their adverse AMs (e.g., affect, specificity, integrative meaning), and the way in which patients narrate their life story before and after treatment. It can do this by using tools such as the Big Five Inventory for assessing personality traits (John & Srivastava, 1999); the personal goals measure (e.g., Emmons, 1986); memory coding manuals (e.g., Singer & Blagov, 2000); and the life story interview (McAdams, 1993), which can be used to understand how patients narrate their life and how this may change following treatment. State measures of affect and self-esteem, as well as behavioural tasks, could help us to understand how the targeted memories affect patients when retrieved before and after treatment. This kind of research would provide a more comprehensive view of the changes that cognitive-behavioural interventions promote. This view, combined with the existing literature on what constitutes a healthy memory system and personality, can help identify the areas in which these interventions need improving. If, for example, interventions such as ImRs are successful in modifying the targeted memories but do not promote overall changes in patients' life story, we can combine them with elements of life review interventions (see Chapter 5). We can then compare the effectiveness of the combined intervention to that of ImRs used on its own, particularly in producing lasting changes and preventing relapse.

The narrative identity literature can also help us understand novel interventions, such as those involving visuospatial tasks or propranolol. As mentioned earlier, to date we know only one main outcome for each of these interventions: reduction of intrusions for Tetris and reduction of the memory's affective charge for propranolol. There are thus several questions that future research needs to address. How do these interventions influence the meaning making process? What are their implications for how the targeted AMs contribute to the life story and sense of self? Can dampened affect following propranolol administration facilitate meaning making or can it distort it by not allowing individuals to accurately assess the relevance of the experience (e.g., the threat posed by it)? As reconsolidation disruption interventions are simple and can promote change relatively rapidly, they offer significant promise for use in therapeutic settings. Understanding how they work and what potential long-term effects they can have, however, is essential.

Conclusion

As we conclude this book, we hope to have achieved our aim of demonstrating how cognitive, social, personality, and clinical psychology can contribute to our understanding of AM and its relevance for clinical practice. The research in this area is rapidly growing. In fact, while working on the book we sometimes had to re-write entire sections because of new research that was being published. A good part of the recently published articles do cross the disciplinary boundaries as they explore or at least acknowledge the implications of the research for other disciplines. However, we feel that greater communication is needed. We acknowledge that it may be difficult for researchers and practitioners to keep up with the volume of work that is being published in disciplines outside their own. This may be even more difficult for clinicians dealing with high caseloads and other pressures related to their practice. By synthesising the key research in this book and proposing ways in which the different disciplines can inform each other, we hope to update professionals about recent developments and to encourage further interdisciplinary research. Like Singer and Salovey (1993), we "do not believe that truth can be found if each subdiscipline of psychology tends its own garden" (p. 215). We also believe that at this time the various disciplines cannot afford to tend their own gardens. With pressure to develop cost-effective treatments in struggling mental health services, as well as worldwide social and economic unrest, it is essential that as psychologists we step up and utilise the knowledge about human beings we have accumulated in the past century to enhance the therapeutic support we provide. By obtaining a comprehensive answer to the question *"Who am I?"* through research, we can train clinicians so they can provide a more profound, better-informed answer to the questions *"Who are you? And how can I best help you?"*

References

Adler, J. M., Lodi-Smith, J., Philippe, F. L., & Houle, I. (2016). The incremental validity of narrative identity in predicting well-being: A review of the field and recommendations for the future. *Personality and Social Psychology Review, 20*(2), 142–175.

Alea, N. (2018). Does the life story interview make us make sense? Spontaneous and cued redemption and contamination in life story scenes. *Imagination, Cognition and Personality, 37*(3), 271–292.

Beckers, T. & Kindt, M. (2017). Memory reconsolidation interference as an emerging treatment for emotional disorders: Strengths, limitations, challenges, and opportunities. *Annual Review of Clinical Psychology, 13*, 99–121.

Berntsen, D. & Rubin, D. C. (2014). Involuntary memories and dissociative amnesia: Assessing key assumptions in posttraumatic stress disorder research. *Clinical Psychological Science, 2*(2), 174–186.

Bluck, S. (2017). Remember and review or forget and let go? Views from a functional approach to autobiographical memory. *The International Journal of Reminiscence and Life Review, 4*(1), 3–7.

Brewin, C. R. (2016). Coherence, disorganization, and fragmentation in traumatic memory reconsidered: A response to Rubin et al. (2016). *Journal of Abnormal Psychology, 125*(7), 1011–1017.

Crespo, M. & Fernández-Lansac, V. (2016). Memory and narrative of traumatic events: A literature review. *Psychological Trauma: Theory, Research, Practice, and Policy, 8*, 149–156.

Elsey, J. W. B. & Kindt, M. (2017). Tackling maladaptive memories through reconsolidation: From neural to clinical science. *Neurobiology of Learning and Memory, 142*, 108–117.

Emmons, R. A. (1986). Personal strivings: An approach to personality and subjective well-being. *Journal of Personality and Social Psychology, 51*(5), 1058–1068.

Graci, M. E., Watts, A. L., & Fivush, R. (2018). Examining the factor structure of narrative meaning-making for stressful events and relations with psychological distress. *Memory*. Advance online publication.

Gregory, B., Wong, Q. J. J., Marker, C. D., & Peters, L. (2018). Maladaptive self-beliefs during cognitive behavioural therapy for social anxiety disorder: A test of temporal precedence. *Cognitive Therapy and Research, 42*(3), 261–272.

Hagenaars, M. A., Holmes, E. A., Klaassen, F., & Elzinga, B. (2017). Tetris and Word games lead to fewer intrusive memories when applied several days after analogue trauma. *European Journal of Psychotraumatology, 8*, 1386959.

Holm, T. & Thomsen, D. K. (2018). Self-event connections in life stories, self-concept clarity, and dissociation: Examining their relations with symptoms of psychopathology. *Imagination, Cognition and Personality, 37*(3), 293–317.

Horsch, A., Vial, Y., Favrod, C., Harari, M. M., Blackwell, S. E., et al. (2017). Reducing intrusive traumatic memories after emergency caesarean section: A proof-of-principle randomized controlled study. *Behaviour Research and Therapy, 94*, 36–47.

Iyadurai, L., Blackwell, S. E., Meiser-Stedman, R., Watson, P. C., Bonsall, M. B., et al. (2018). Preventing intrusive memories after trauma via a brief intervention involving Tetris computer game play in the emergency department: A proof-of-concept randomized controlled trial. *Molecular Psychiatry, 23*(3), 674–682.

John, O. P. & Srivastava, S. (1999). The Big-Five trait taxonomy: History, measurement, and theoretical perspectives. In L. A. Pervin & O. P. John (Eds.), *Handbook of personality: Theory and research* (Vol. 2, pp. 102–138). New York, NY: Guilford Press.

Kindt, M. (2018). The surprising subtleties of changing fear memory: A challenge for translational science. *Philosophical Transactions B: Royal Society, 373*, 20170033.

Kindt, M. & van Emmerik, A. (2016). New avenues for treating emotional memory disorders: Towards a reconsolidation intervention for posttraumatic stress disorder. *Therapeutic Advances in Psychopharmacology, 6*(4), 283–295.

McAdams, D. P. (1993). *The stories we live by: Personal myths and the making of the self.* New York, NY: William Morrow.

McAdams, D. P. (2015). Three lines of personality development: A conceptual itinerary. *European Psychologist, 20*(4), 252–264.

McLean, K. C. & Fournier, M. A. (2008). The content and processes of autobiographical reasoning in narrative identity. *Journal of Research in Personality, 42*, 527–545.

Oppenheim, M. (2016, April 5). Sir Ian McKellen returns advance rumoured to be worth £1 million for his memoirs due to painful memories. *The Independent*. Retrieved from www.independent.co.uk

O'Toole, M. S., Watson, L., Rosenberg, N. K., & Berntsen, D. (2018). Changes in perceived centrality of anxious events following cognitive behavioral therapy for social anxiety disorder and panic disorder. *Journal of Behavior Therapy and Experimental Psychiatry, 59*, 150–156.

Panattoni, K. & McLean, K. C. (2018). The curious case of the coding and self-ratings mismatches: A methodological and theoretical detective story. *Imagination, Cognition and Personality, 37*(3), 248–270.

Park, C. L. (2010). Making sense of the meaning literature: An integrative review of meaning making and its effects on adjustment to stressful life events. *Psychological Bulletin, 136*(2), 257–301.

Rubin, D. C., Berntsen, D., Ogle, C. M., Deffler, S. A., & Beckham, J. C. (2016). Scientific evidence versus outdated beliefs: A response to Brewin (2016). *Journal of Abnormal Psychology, 125*, 1018–1021.

Singer, J. A. (2005). *Personality and psychotherapy: Treating the whole person.* New York, NY: Guilford Press.

Singer, J. A. & Blagov, P. S. (2000). *Classification system and scoring manual for self-defining autobiographical memories.* Unpublished manuscript, Department of Psychology, Connecticut College, New London, CT.

Singer, J. A. & Salovey, P. (1993). *The remembered self: Emotion and memory in personality.* New York, NY: Free Press.

Westerhof, G. J. (2017). Technologies to remember or forget? A perspective from reminiscence and life review. *The International Journal of Reminiscence and Life Review, 4*(1), 8–13.

Index

actual self 28
adaptive correspondence 39, 47
affect: associated with intrusive
    mental images 76–78; proposed
    changes following cognitive-
    behavioural interventions
    103–106; relation to goals and need
    satisfaction 29, 40; relevance for
    psychological well-being 56–57,
    66–67, 69; in response to memory
    retrieval 39–41, 47; in self-defining
    memories 31; *see also* emotion
agency 20; following administration
    of memory-focused cognitive-
    behavioural interventions 104–105;
    and psychological well-being
    57–58, 67
AM *see* autobiographical memory
autobiographical memory (AM): in
    cognitive-behavioural therapy
    94–99, 102–106; cultural differences
    6–8, 44–45; definition of 1;
    functions of 1–5; impact of retrieval
    39–44; as origin of intrusive mental
    images 75–76; and the life story
    18–22, 25–26; in the self-memory
    system model 26–29, 46–49
autobiographical reasoning 19–22,
    67, 103–104, 107; in relation
    to age and culture 22–25;
    see also meaning making
autonoesis 1, 46

Berntsen, D. 4, 6, 39, 56–57, 62–64, 102
borderline personality disorder
    (BPD) 58, 64–65, 70–71, 94

BPD *see* borderline personality
    disorder
Brewin, C. R. 62–64, 72–74, 76,
    100–101

causal coherence 20, 64, 68–69, 103
CBT *see* cognitive-behavioural
    therapy
cognitive model 94, 103
cognitive-behavioural therapy (CBT)
    93–94, 107–109, 118–119, 121;
    effectiveness of 98–99; focusing on
    adverse memories and intrusive
    images 94–98; mechanisms of
    change in 99–100; mechanisms of
    change from a narrative identity
    perspective 102–106
coherent positive resolution 61–62,
    67, 104
communion 20; and psychological
    well-being 57, 67
contamination sequences 21; and
    psychological well-being 41,
    58–59
Conway, M. A. 17, 25–31, 47–48, 62,
    65, 103
core beliefs 94–95, 102, 107
cultural coherence 20
cultural life script 24, 62
culture: and autobiographical
    reasoning 23–25; and the impact
    of autobiographical memory
    retrieval 44–45; and the importance
    of narrative structure for
    psychological well-being 63; and
    memory functions 6–8

depression 10, 45, 56–59, 61, 63–65, 70–73, 75, 77, 99, 109
dispositional traits 17; changes following cognitive-behavioural therapy 103, 105; in the life story model 18; and self-event connections 22
dysphoria 45, 64

emotion 4–5, 28–29, 31, 39–41, 74, 96–97; *see also* affect

FAB *see* fading affect bias
fading affect bias (FAB) 40

generativity 4, 59
goals: changes following cognitive-behavioural therapy 103–106; definition of 26; and impact of memory retrieval 40, 42–43, 47–49; in the life story model 17–18; and memory retention 29–31; in relation to meaning making and psychological well-being 67–71; in self-defining memories 31; in the self-memory system model 26–28

Habermas, T. 19–20, 23–25, 60, 67

ideal self 28–29
imagery rescripting (ImRs) 96–99, 101, 104, 106
imaginal reliving (IR) 97, 104
ImRs *see* imagery rescripting
intrusive mental images: characteristics of 72–75; origin of 75–76; role in the onset and maintenance of psychological disorders 76–79
involuntary memory 6, 41, 45, 72
IR *see* imaginal reliving

life review 108–109
life-review therapy 108–109
life story model of personality development 18–19; in relation to mechanisms of change in cognitive-behavioural therapy 103–106

life story schema 19, 27
long-term self 17, 27–28, 30, 47, 78, 103

master narratives 23–25, 58–60
McAdams, D. P. 17–19, 21, 23, 25, 59, 102–103, 121
McLean, K. C. 2, 6, 19–21, 23–25, 59–60, 117–118
meaning making 19; issues with assessment 117–118; and psychological well-being 57–62, 67–69; in therapy 102
memory specificity 31, 40, 64–65; *see also* overgeneral retrieval

narrative exposure therapy (NET) 108–109
narrative identity 2–3, 17, 19; in cognitive-behavioural therapy 102–104, 106–108, 121–122
NET *see* narrative exposure therapy

ought self 28–29
overgeneral memory 64–65, 70; *see also* memory specificity
overgeneral retrieval 65–66, 68, 70–71, 98, 102; *see also* overgeneral memory

PE *see* prolonged exposure
personality 17, 21–22; and memory functions 9–10; proposed changes following cognitive-behavioural therapy 103–106; *see also* life story model of personality development
posttraumatic stress disorder (PTSD) 56–58, 62–65, 70–72, 73, 75, 78, 97–99
prolonged exposure (PE) 96, 98, 100
propranolol 119–120, 122
psychosis 74–77, 99
PTSD *see* posttraumatic stress disorder

redemption 24, 102, 104–105
redemption sequences 21; and psychological well-being 58–60

schizophrenia 56–57, 60, 64–65, 68, 71
SDMs *see* self-defining memories

self: changes in cognitive-behavioural therapy 100–102; definitions of 17–18; development of 18–22, 25–26, 30–31, 66–68; impact of memory retrieval on 41–42; and intrusive mental images 76; in the self-memory system model 26–28
self-concept clarity 9, 56, 67, 78
self-defining memories (SDMs): characteristics and dimensions of 31–32; in cognitive-behavioural therapy 103–107; impact of retrieval 40–43, 49; and psychological well-being 60–61, 64–66, 68–69, 71
self-esteem 9–10, 41–42, 56, 59, 61, 63, 66–67
self-event connections 21–22, 60–61, 67, 103–105
self-images 28, 30, 47–49, 67, 78
self-memory system model (SMS) 26–31, 38–39, 46–49, 62, 78

Singer, J. A. 19–21, 31–32, 68–70, 102, 107, 121
SMS model *see* self-memory system model
social anxiety disorder 56, 72–75, 77, 95, 99–102
structural master narratives 24–25

Tetris 119–120, 122
Trauma: and overgeneral retrieval 65–66; and psychopathology 56, 73–74; and PTSD 58, 62–64, 70, 75; related goals 69–70; therapeutic interventions for 96–98, 119
temporal coherence 20, 63–64
thematic coherence 20, 22, 63, 103–104
Thomsen, D. K. 56–57, 60–61, 67, 117

working self 27–28, 30, 39, 47, 49, 78

For Product Safety Concerns and Information please contact our EU representative GPSR@taylorandfrancis.com Taylor & Francis Verlag GmbH, Kaufingerstraße 24, 80331 München, Germany

Printed and bound by CPI Group (UK) Ltd, Croydon, CR0 4YY

11/04/2025

01843992-0005